TITA
HALIFAX

D1246151

NIMBUS
PUBLISHING LTD

Titanic Halifax
Alan Jeffers and Rob Gordon

Copyright © Alan Jeffers and
Rob Gordon, 1998

Nimbus Publishing Limited
PO Box 9301, Station A
Halifax, Nova Scotia, Canada
B3K 5N5
(902) 455-4286

Design: Arthur Carter, Halifax
Cover captions: Halifax skyline
and Fairview Cemetery.

Printed and bound by
Printcrafters Inc.

Canadian Cataloguing in
Publication Data
Jeffers, Alan, 1958-
Titanic Halifax
ISBN 1-55109-275-1
1. Halifax (N.S.) — Guidebooks.
2. Titanic (Steamship)
I.Gordon, Robert, 1954-
II. Title.
FC2346.18.J43 1998
917.1'6'225   C98-950122-1
F1039.5H17J43 1998.

Nimbus Publishing
acknowledges the financial
support of the Canada Council
and the Department of
Canadian Heritage.

Most historic images in this publica-
tion are available from the National
Archives of Canada, the Halifax
Regional Library, Nova Scotia
Legislative Library, Maritime
Command Museum, Dalhousie
University Library, Saint Mary's
University Library, and the Public
Record Office, London.

The following images are from the
Public Archives of Nova Scotia:
p. xi: A.B. Siteman, 31-4-7; p. 1T:
Notman #66919; p. 1 B: Snow's
Funeral Home #1, 33-5-5; p. 5 T:
Ships & Shipping: Titanic No 2,
PANS N-0715, 51-2; p. 8: Notman #
16, PANS N-2332 or N-5484; p. 9 B:
Ships & Shipping: Titanic No 1,
PANS 0715, 51-2; p. 12: Ships &
Shipping: Montmagny PANS N-
5481, 51-2; p. 19 T: Halifax Post
cards: 1895-1955, 31-4-7; p. 19 B:
Places: Halifax: Hotels, 53-3; p.22:
Joseph S Rogers # 44, PANS N- 0717,
31-2-3; p. 26 B: Notman #70639,
PANS N-7443; p.27 B: Annabelle
Siteman Ells, #68, 36-1-1; p. 29: RG
41 Series "C" Volume 76, #236
p. 58 T: "Halifax and its Attractions"
(1902), Howard & Kutsche; p. 60 T:
Notman #1113, PANS N-5142; p. 67:
Fader #6, PANS N-6208, 31-2-4;
p. 69: Carriages: Snow & Co., PANS
N-0714, 54.4; p. 73: Notman #4128,
PANS N-4127; p. 74 B: "Halifax and
its Attractions" (1902), Howard &
Kutsche; p. 76: RG41 Series "C"
Vol.76, No 124; p. 77 T: Ships &
Shipping: Atlantic, Bollinger #5254,
51-2; p. 77 C: Ships & Shipping:
Atlantic, PANS N-0727, 51-2; p. 77 B:
Ships & Shipping: Imo, PANS N-
0138, 51-2; p. 93: Snow's Funeral
Home # 2, PANS N-3831, 33-5-5

Maritime Museum of the Atlantic
contributed images of their Titanic
artifacts, including items on loan
from the Department of Canadian
Heritage and Public Archives of
Nova Scotia. These items were pho-
tographed by Jamie Steeves, Derek
Harrison, and Roger Lloyd.

Recent images were provided by the
authors and Arthur Carter; the
colour photo on page 58 was taken
by Albert Lee.

Contents

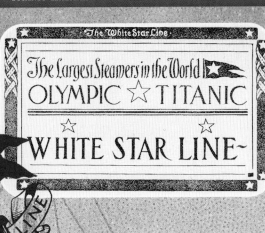

INTRODUCTION: SINKING OF THE TITANIC

It was never meant to be, but Halifax became the final destination for many of the passengers aboard *Titanic* on her maiden voyage that ended tragically on April 14, 1912.

Today, traces of the disaster can be found on Halifax streets, on docks, and in graveyards, where the remains of 150 victims of one of the world's greatest tragedies lie. Halifax shouldn't have had this tragic link with *Titanic*—a connection that was renewed when writer-director James Cameron chose the city

Halifax as viewed from the Citadel c1912.

to film modern-day scenes for the block-buster movie "Titanic," but fate intervened.

When the then world's largest ship sailed from Southampton, England, for New York in 1912, there were only two prominent Halifax residents aboard— millionaire George Wright and Hilda Slayter, an upper-class young woman who had been to England to prepare for her wedding. The ship was bound for

Opposite: White Star logo, advertisement and detail from a contemporary post card illustrating the *Titanic*.

New York, nine hundred miles south of Halifax on the Eastern Seaboard of the United States.

Fate brought Halifax and *Titanic* together when the ship that was considered unsinkable met her end after colliding with an iceberg, seven hundred miles east of the city.

The first connection between *Titanic* and Halifax began as a result of an unfortunate mistake moments after the tragedy began. Initial wireless messages were garbled and transposed, misleading the world into believing that all passengers and crew of *Titanic* were safe and on their way to Halifax.

It's thought that a ship in the area, *Baltic*, sent out the following message on its wireless: "Are all *Titanic* passengers safe?" At the same time, another ship, *Asian*, sent out a message indicating she was towing a disabled tanker, *Deutschland*, to Halifax. The resulting message was picked up as: "*Titanic* passengers safe; being towed to Halifax," but the information was horribly wrong.

Newspapers jumped the gun and reported that agents for the White Star Line, owner of the *Titanic*, had sent tugs to escort *Titanic* to port. White Star was later accused of fuelling the misunderstanding with false statements about *Titanic*'s fate.

The *Halifax Morning Chronicle* was still breathing a sigh of relief in its April 15th edition, a full day after the sinking. It reported "...that all the passengers has [sic] been safely taken off and were on their way to Halifax on board three steamers [that had been in the area], the Allan liners *Virginian* and *Parisian* and the Cunard liner *Carpathia*. In view of

An article that appeared in the *Daily Mail*, London.

LAST OF THE TITANIC.

SUNK LAST NIGHT.

NO LIVES LOST.

NEW YORK, Monday.
The Titanic sank at 2.20 this afternoon.
No lives were lost,—Reuter.

OPERATOR'S DIARY.
From Our Own Correspondent.
HALIFAX, Nova Scotia, Monday.
The work of transferring the passengers to the Carpathia was carried out under favourable circumstances, the weather being fairly moderate.

A report from the *Christian Science Monitor*.

PASSENGERS SAFELY MOVED AND STEAMER TITANIC TAKEN IN TOW

Carpathia and Parisian Care for Those Aboard Disabled Liner While Virginian Lends Aid to Make Port

BULKHEADS HOLD

Officials of White Star Company Confident Steamer Is Unsinkable and Will Float Until Halifax Is Reached

Top opposite page: *Boston Globe* Headline.

this fact the officials of the Intercolonial [Railway] at once began making arrangements for the forwarding of passengers to New York. Extra cars for the making up of special trains were being gathered together from various railroads for the purpose and were dispatched to Halifax."

Immigration officials sent inspectors to Halifax to speed processing of *Titanic* passengers. Other special trains were dispatched from New York to Nova Scotia to bring relieved friends and relatives to meet the ship.

But by the time the newspaper hit the streets, the shocking truth had become known. The welcoming plans in Halifax were cancelled, the train turned around in Maine, and the custom officials were sent home.

(Ironically, even two days after the sinking, a report in the April 16 London *Daily Sketch* still provided completely erroneous information.

"Though the sea was pouring into the vessel forward, her machinery had not been disabled. It was found that, with the pumps working and the watertight bulkheads holding well, there was a good chance of the liner making port, and the captain proceeded slowly and cautiously in the direction of Halifax, notifying his intention to the vessels already hurrying to his aid.")

RMS Titanic at dock in Southampton.

News of the disaster had arrived from the steamship *Carpathia* which had responded to *Titanic*'s distress call. *Carpathia* had zigged and zagged fifty-eight miles through ice-infested waters to reach the coordinates received from *Titanic*'s wireless operators. There they found *Titanic*'s lifeboats, filled with 705 shiver-

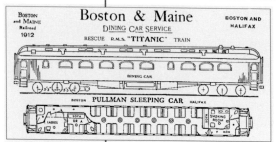

A Boston and Maine Railroad advertisement for the "Rescue R.M.S. Titanic Train" from Boston to Halifax.

ing and shaken survivors. But all that was left of the great ship itself was flotsam and jetsam. *Carpathia* was far too late for *Titanic*'s dead—1,523 had perished in the icy North Atlantic.

The survivors were quickly taken aboard the *Carpathia* which arrived in New York on April 18. The grim task of locating *Titanic*'s victims fell to Halifax. White Star's agent in the bustling port city, A. G. Jones, chartered the steamship *Mackay-Bennett*, which normally laid and repaired telegraph cables on

The New York Times reveals the true story.

the ocean floor, to make her way to *Titanic*'s last-known location to search for and retrieve bodies.

The ship, crewed by Nova Scotians from across the province, was loaded with clergy, undertakers, coffins, and ice and set off on its unhappy voyage. It took them three days to travel the seven hundred miles to the site of the wreck. What they found was unimaginable.

"As far as the eye can see, the ocean was strewn with wreckage and debris," a horrified crewman, Arminias Wiseman, recalled later. "Bodies [were] bobbing up and down in the cold sea."

Mackay-Bennett found so many bodies—306 in all—that the crew had to hail a passing ship and ask for extra burlap and canvas to cover the dead. Another cable ship from Halifax, *Minia*,

joined *Mackay-Bennett* after nine days at sea to resupply her with embalming fluid and continue the search while the first load of bodies was taken to Halifax.

By now, Halifax was a city in mourning, awaiting the "Death Ship," as *Mackay-Bennett* was dubbed by the sensationalist newspapers of the day. Black bunting was hung everywhere in Halifax. Relatives of the dead were rushing in from all over, making the city a centre of anguish and loss. Pictures of *Titanic* surrounded by black were featured in the windows of stores and other businesses in the downtown. Men and women spoke in hushed tones. Church bells pealed for the dead.

Finally, the "Death Ship" arrived in port.

Mackay-Bennett didn't dock at her regular berth, at Karlsen Wharf, just north of the Sheraton Hotel and Casino. For security reasons and out of respect for the dead,

The rescue ship *Carpathia*.

Titanic lifeboats No, 14 and collapsible D, pictured from *Carpathia*.

it was decided that she would steam an extra mile north in the harbour to the Naval Dockyard's North Coaling Wharf No. 4 for unloading.

The location was perfect. A high concrete wall would keep out prying eyes. Navy crewmen could guard the site. Churchgoers had been urged during Sunday services on April 28 to stay away from the area. Bodies were carried from the ship on stretchers and placed into

Various business throughout Halifax displayed pictures of the *Titanic*, draped in purple and black bunting in honour of the dead.

horse-drawn hearses. The thirty hearses then travelled a half-mile to the Mayflower Curling Rink, where a makeshift morgue had been hastily assembled.

Soon Halifax's churches would fill with mourners; three graveyards would be home to *Titanic*'s dead.

No one could have guessed that *Titanic*'s maiden voyage would end in disaster and tragedy when the world's most luxurious liner slipped her lines in Southampton near London on April 10, 1912. Excitement and awe were the predominant feelings as her giant propellers churned the water, pushing the monstrous 46,328 ton hull away from land forever.

Titanic's end began with her launching a year earlier, on May 31, 1911 at the Hartland and Woolf shipyard in Belfast. That's when the work of fifteen thousand shipyard workers was finally completed and the great ship slipped down the builder's ways and into water for the first time. The shipyard workers had been assigned one task by the White Star Line: Create the largest, most opulent steamship of the day.

Never before had a ship encompassed such luxury. Never before had a ship been designed to carry so many poor immigrants from Europe's ghettos to the hopes and dreams of America.

The luxury was meant for the rich, who could afford it. As *Titanic*'s bow pointed west towards the open waters of the Atlantic, her upper deck carried some of the world's wealthiest men. They included U.S. industrialist John Jacob Astor; J. Bruce Ismay, the chairman of the White Star Line who prided himself on always taking the maiden voyage on the line's new ships; and

Halifax's Barrington Street c1912. The building fourth from the left was owned by *Titanic* victim, George Wright.

Barrington Street, North from Sackville St., Halifax, N.S.

Charles M. Hays, president of the Montreal-based Grand Trunk Railway.

For the lower deck passengers, *Titanic* meant passage to a new world. What many of these immigrants did not know was that life in the so-called new world was organized pretty much as was life aboard *Titanic*. For instance, Halifax in 1912 was divided along class and religious lines. George Wright, the Halifax businessman who died aboard *Titanic*, was a progressive man who was trying to break down the social barriers of the day—the very social system the giant ship embodied. Wright created a revolutionary housing development on South Park Street in Halifax's South End which mixed and mingled the classes, something that was unheard of at the time. The development, which still stands today, featured turreted mansions for the rich, more modest homes for Halifax's growing middle class, and row houses for the working poor.

TITANIC SHIP FACTS

★ *Titanic* was 883 ft. long on deck, almost one-sixth of a mile. She was 92 ft. wide and weighed 46,328 tons, about half the weight of a modern U.S. aircraft carrier. From the bottom of her keel to the top of her bridge, *Titanic* was 104 ft. tall.

★ When *Titanic* sank on April 14, 1912, she was the largest moveable object built in human history.

★ *Titanic's* hull was made of one-inch thick steel, which turned out to be extremely brittle because of high sulphur content. *Titanic* was divided into sixteen watertight compartments. This design is thought to have originated the claim that she was unsinkable.

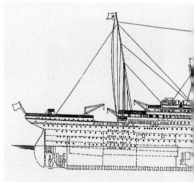

Among the lower-class passengers aboard *Titanic* were Swedish immigrant Alma Paulson and her four children. They had saved enough money to book third-class passage to join her husband, Nils, in Chicago and start a new life. Paulson's fair-haired two-year-old boy, Gosta, would become *Titanic's* "Unknown Child" whose plight would touch the hearts of thousands.

In second class was the fugitive Michel Navratil who purchased a ticket under the name Louis Hoffman to spirit his sons away from his failing marriage. Like so many, Navratil died courageously to save the lives of his two young sons, who became the mysterious "Orphans of the *Titanic*" until their frantic mother saw their photograph in newspapers in France.

There was yet another world below decks. Down in the sweltering, filthy engine room, men like twenty-three-year-old James Dawson hauled coal to the stokers who fired *Titanic*'s massive boilers. Dawson was a poor Irishman who managed to secure a job as a trimmer aboard the ship just days before she left her home port of Southampton, southwest of London. No one could have imagined that his name would be given

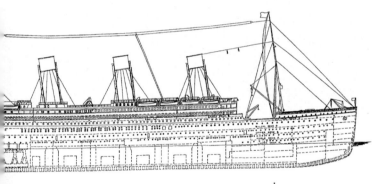

to a fictional character in an award-winning feature film about *Titanic* three-quarters of a century later, or that his grave in Halifax would become a mecca for tourists.

There were 2,228 people aboard *Titanic* as she began her maiden voyage on April 10, 1912. In just a few days, Astor, Paulson, Navratil, Dawson, and hundreds of others, regardless of class, would share a fate they could never have imagined. Although unequal in life, in a few short hours they would be equal in death.

A drawing of the *Titanic*.

RECOVERING THE DEAD

When news of *Titanic's* sinking and loss of life made its way to Halifax, the city answered the call. The White Star Line, owners of *Titanic*, used their Halifax agents, A. G. Jones, to charter *Mackay-Bennett* from her owners, the Commercial Cable Company. Almost immediately, the crew of the *Mackay-Bennett* began preparations to travel the seven hundred miles across the icy North Atlantic to begin the grim search for *Titanic's* dead. *Mackay-Bennett* was a steam-driven cable ship, meant for laying and repairing transatlantic telegraph cables.

Now she had a very different job. She would become a floating morgue, her cable-lifting crane taking on the unfamiliar task of pulling bodies from the Atlantic. For this work she came to be referred to as the "Death Ship."

White Star Line also hired John Snow and Company Ltd., the largest undertaking firm in Nova Scotia, to prepare the recovered bodies for burial. Soon, more than one hundred rough-hewn wooden coffins lined the wharf on Halifax's waterfront at what is now known as Karlsen Wharf, just north of the Sheraton Hotel and Casino.

Under the supervision of Captain F. H. Lardner the coffins were loaded on *Mackay-Bennett's* deck. Tons of ice were delivered on quick order from a local icehouse. Containers of embalming fluid were assembled. Canvas sacks and scrap iron to weigh down bodies for burial at

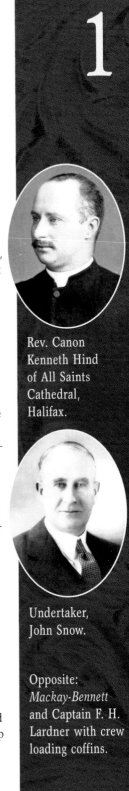

Rev. Canon Kenneth Hind of All Saints Cathedral, Halifax.

Undertaker, John Snow.

Opposite: *Mackay-Bennett* and Captain F. H. Lardner with crew loading coffins.

sea were put on board. The ship's seventy-five officers and crew from across Nova Scotia prepared for the worst. Canon Kenneth O. Hind from All Saints Cathedral in Halifax joined the crew for spiritual duty.

Mackay-Bennett left Halifax just after noon Wednesday, April 17—three days after the sinking—on what would turn out to be a thirteen day return journey filled with horror. The ship left port at full speed but only ninety minutes out had to slow down due to rough weather and fog.

An iceberg as seen by passing ships days after the sinking of the *Titanic*.

Three days later, after maneuvering around icebergs that towered above the ship, the *Mackay-Bennett* reached the general area of *Titanic's* last known position. Lardner requested that other ships, which had recently passed through the area, report what they had found, and there was no shortage of gruesome stories.

Johanna Stunke, a first-class passenger aboard the North German Lloyd liner *Bremen*, which had just passed by *Titanic's* grave on the way to New York, described the scene: "We saw the body of one woman in only her nightdress and clasping a baby to her breast. Close by was the body of another woman with her arms tightly clasped round a shaggy dog. We saw the bodies of three men in a group, all clinging to a chair. Floating by just beyond them were the bodies of a dozen men, all wearing life belts and clinging desperately together as though in their last struggle for life."

British journalist and educator, William Stead was lost in the disaster.

Stunke and the others aboard *Bremen* had begged the officers to stop to pick up the bodies but were assured that *Mackay-Bennett* was on her way. Although the *Mackay-Bennett* was in position about 8:00 P.M. on the evening of Saturday, April 20, it was too dark to search. Captain Lardner ordered the ship to drift until morning.

By the middle of the night, bodies and wreckage had been sighted.

At daylight, smaller boats were dropped into the water and the grim job of recovering the victims began. Fifty-one of *Titanic's* dead were recovered Sunday, April 21, including a mysterious little blond-haired boy—the fourth body recovered—who later became known as the "Unknown Child" of *Titanic*.

The fifteenth body recovered that day was Michel Navratil, the fugitive from France who had been travelling under the assumed name of Louis Hoffman in an attempt to take his two sons to America, away from his estranged wife.

As the bodies were lifted from the small boats to the *Mackay-Bennett*, a simple but effective procedure, developed by John Barnstead, deputy registrar of death, was repeatedly carried out. A piece of canvas with a stencilled number on it was attached to each body to indicate the order in which it was recovered from the water. In a ledger, a detailed entry described hair colour, height, weight, approximate age, and any obvious markings on the body. This simple record would prove invaluable when the difficult job of identifying *Titanic's* victims began in Halifax.

With a witness present, an inventory was taken—contents of pockets, money, jewellery, and clothing; all would provide valuable clues in the days, even years, ahead. Any property found was placed in a canvas bag which was numbered corresponding to the

TITANIC BODY RECOVERY FACTS

★ Bodies of first-class passengers found at sea were embalmed and placed in coffins aboard the recovery vessels. Second-and third-class passengers were placed in canvas bags. Steerage passengers and crew members were placed on piles of ice in the vessels' bow.

★ Three hundred twenty-eight bodies were recovered at sea; 119 bodies were too damaged in the tragedy to preserve and were buried at sea in canvas bags weighted down with iron rods and other bits of scrap iron.

The family of Philadelphia millionaire George Widener came to Halifax to claim his body when the *Mackay-Bennett* returned. The body was not found. His wife, Eleanor (below), survived.

The body of Francis Millet, an artist and raconteur, was recovered by the *Mackay-Bennett* and later sent to the United States.

number given each body. *Titanic* graves in Halifax today still bear those numbers.

The same numbering system would be used again five years later in the aftermath of the Halifax Explosion, in which the munitions ship *Mont Blanc* exploded, killing more than sixteen hundred people and flattening the North End of Halifax.

Mackay-Bennett's small boats returned with their cargo by sundown on the first day of body recovery. On the forecastle deck, Canon Hind conducted a service for twenty-four unidentified bodies, mostly crew members who were badly disfigured, before they were buried at sea.

The following morning at 5:30 A.M. the macabre task began anew.

There was wreckage as far as the eye could see. *Mackay-Bennett* came across *Titanic* lifeboat Collapsible B, which was found overturned with a gaping hole in one side. More bodies were recovered.

By now supplies were beginning to run low. *Mackay-Bennett* sent a message to a passing steamer and secured badly needed burlap and canvas to enclose the bodies. More and more of *Titanic's* dead were being pulled from the ocean and the supply of embalming fluid was running low.

"All not embalmed will be buried at sea at 8:00 P.M. with divine services," Captain Lardner said in a message to shore on Thursday, April 25. "Can only bring embalmed bodies to port."

On April 21, the White Star Line had realized that *Mackay-Bennett* couldn't handle the number of dead alone. So, its Halifax agents, A. G. Jones, chartered another cable ship, the *Minia*, owned by the Anglo-American Telegraph Company Ltd. to provide assistance. *Minia's* captain was W. G. S. DeCarteret, ironically a tenant of George Wright, the only Halifax native to die aboard *Titanic*.

White Star wanted DeCarteret and the *Minia* to leave port by 4:00 P.M. on Monday, April 22, but there was a problem—a shortage of coffins. John Snow and Company undertakers contacted the James Dempster Company Ltd., a local coffin manufacturer, and the factory operated through the afternoon and into the evening to fill the order.

Embalming a body on the deck of the *Minia*.

Like the *Mackay-Bennett*, the *Minia* took along a clergyman, the Rev. H. W. Cunningham of St. George's Anglican Church—also known as the Round Church—and undertaker H. W. Snow. Also on board was an extra supply of embalming fluid, 150 coffins and 10 tons of iron bars to weigh down the dead for burial at sea. Twenty tons of ice were dumped on the one hundred miles of cable in the hold. There wasn't time to remove it before *Minia* left port, just before midnight.

DIARY OF CREW MEMBER ABOARD MACKAY-BENNETT

This is the only known first-hand account of the cable ship *Mackay-Bennett's* thirteen-day journey to recover *Titanic's* dead. This diary was kept by a

The *Mackay-Bennett* recovered the body of Major Archibald Butt, military aide to U.S. President Taft.

Col. John Jacob Astor, believed to be the richest man in the world, and his wife Madeleine. J.J. Astor's body was brought to Halifax and sent to the United States by train for burial. His young wife survived the disaster.

BODIES OF ASTOR AND STRAUS ARE FOUND AT SEA

Steamer Mackey Bennett Coming to Port With Remains of Noted Men Picked Up at Scene of Titanic Disaster. Ninety-One of Two Hundred and Five Bodies Recovered Have Been Identified.

New York, April 26.—The bodies of Colonel Astor, Isidor Straus and Mr. Hays have been recovered from the lost Titanic, according to wireless reports from the steamer, Mackey-Bennett. They were found floating in life belts near where the White Star liner went down.

It is hoped that the body of Maj. Archie Butt may yet be recognized among the bodies recovered.

Ninety-one of the two hundred and five bodies recovered have been completely identified.

member of the steamship's crew and published in the April 30, 1912, edition of the *Halifax Evening News*. The name of the crew member, probably from Halifax, wasn't published; however, the events correspond to an account later given reporters by the ship's captain, F. H. Lardner. It's likely that the newspaper paid the man to keep the diary before the ship left Halifax and protected his identity out of fear of retribution from the ship's owners, the Commercial Cable Company.

Wednesday, April 17th: Left Halifax at 12:35 P.M. and steamed full speed out of the harbour. At 1:30 slowed down because of fog. 6:35 P.M. cleared up and went full speed again.

Friday April 19th: At 6:45 picked up a lifebelt with Allan Line marked on it.

Saturday April 20th: Sighted a steamer. Altered course and passed close to her. She reported having seen three large bergs and a number of bodies forty-five miles from the position given by the papers when leaving Halifax. We started off again full speed with a heavy sea running behind us, expecting to reach the spot by 8:00 P.M. At 3:15 passed a large iceberg. At 5:00 P.M. passed a berg about two hundred feet high with some small ice, evidently from large bergs. 7:00 P.M. passed an enormous berg; ran for forty-five minutes and stopped for the night. A lot of wreckage drifting about.

Sunday, April 21st: 5:00 A.M. started steaming for the position of the wreck. At 6:45 picked up the first body, a Danish boy, and during the day picked up fifty-one bodies, four being female, and a child of two or three years, a boy. 5:00 P.M. hoisted boat for the night. Undertaker embalmed twenty bodies, six being left for morning. 8:15 P.M. burial service was held on the forecastle deck when twenty-four bodies were buried, these being mostly of crue [sic] and not identified.

Monday, April 22nd: 5:30 A.M. lowered a boat for a body. Enormous quantity of wreckage. Came upon a lifeboat bottom up, its side smashed in. Steamed away after trying to pick up boat. This day we picked up twenty-seven bodies, Col. John Jacob Astor among them. Everybody had a life belt and bodies floated very high in water in spite of sodden clothes and things in pockets. Apparently people had lots of time, and discipline must have been splendid for some had on their pajamas, two or three shirts, two pairs of pants, two vests, two jackets, and an overcoat. In some pockets a quantity of meat and biscuits were found, while in the pockets of most of the crew quite a lot of tobacco and matches, besides keys to the various lockers and stateroom doors were found. On this day we buried fifteen bodies, some of them very badly smashed and bruised.

Wednesday, April 24th: Heavy sea and very foggy. Could not see a ship's length. The bodies from yesterday were being searched and tagged and stowed away, nobody being buried this day.

Thursday, April 25th: Started at 6:00 A.M. and picked up eighty-seven bodies, keeping them all on board. Bodies searched and tagged in proper order. Heard that cable ship Minia was coming to relieve us. Minia arrived at midnight.

Friday, April 26th: Started again at 6:15 A.M., picked up 6 bodies. Put boat to Minia for embalming fluid. Picked up 8 more bodies, then started for Halifax, having on board 190 bodies. We buried 116 bodies, having picked up 306 all told.

Macy's department store owners Isidor and Ida Strauss both perished. Ida refused to leave her husband's side when given the option of boarding a lifeboat. Isidor's body was recovered and brought to Halifax. His wife's body was not recovered.

RECOVERY SHIP MINIA

After four days of fog and rough weather, *Minia* arrived alongside *Mackay-Bennett* in the early morning of Friday, April 26. At daylight, a small boat transferred the vital embalming fluid to the undertakers aboard *Mackay-Bennett* and the two ships began the search for bod-

The *Minia* as seen in the icy waters of the North Atlantic.

ies together. By noon they had found fourteen more, which were loaded onto *Mackay-Bennett* for her journey back to Halifax.

In just six days, she had found 306 of *Titanic's* dead of which 116 were buried at sea. She headed for Halifax with 190 victims on board, almost twice the number of coffins she carried.

The *Minia* stayed behind but recovered only seventeen more bodies, including that of Charles M. Hays, the Montreal-based president of Grand Trunk Railway.

Francis Dyke, a young crew member who was a temporary wireless operator aboard *Minia*, described the feelings on the ship in the following letter he wrote to his mother while trying to stay awake on the overnight watch.

(Square bracketed words are inserted

where writing was illegible. The original copy of this letter is on display at the Regional Museum of Cultural History in Dartmouth, N.S.)

April 27th/12, 2:20 A.M.

My darling Mother,
I expect you will be surprised to receive this written on this [telegram] paper but I am on watch now in the wireless room so thought it would be a good opportunity to write you. [This is the most] remarkable trip the old Minia has [ever] been on as we are looking for bodies from the Titanic wreck. You know I wrote that we were up north on a cable repair when we heard she had sunk. We arrived in Halifax about three days after and it was reported that we had "some of the rescued on board," but we had not, and the reporters that came to meet us were disappointed.

The same day that we came in, the cable ship Mackay-Bennett of the Commercial Cable Co. was chartered by the White Star (owners) to go out and look for the bodies from the Titanic.

The Mackay-Bennett took 150 coffins and about 20 tons of ice and went to sea at once. Three days after, we were also

New York millionaire, Benjamin Guggenheim did not survive the disaster. He was travelling on the *Titanic* with his Parisian mistress, Madame Aubert, who was among the survivors.

charted by the White Star Co. and we also took 150 coffins and about 20 tons of ice and the same weight of old iron and sailed

A small boat from the *Minia* retrieves a body.

about [1:00 A.M.] on Thursday morning [in] a most rotten fog.

When we arrived (it is about six hundred miles) we found that the Mackay-Bennett had picked up over two hundred bodies and had identified about 150 and had buried the rest. They picked up J. J. Astor's body and some other well-known people. By the way, there was a reward offered of ten thousand dollars for Astor's body, which was lucky for them.

We began the search yesterday and the first we picked up was C. M. Hayes [sic], Pres. of Grand Trunk Rail. It was no trouble to identify him as he had a lot of papers on him and a watch with his name on.

We picked up ten more bodies yesterday (waiters and sailors). All those who are identified are embalmed and packed in ice and are to be sent to New York.

I can tell you none of us like this job at all, but it is better to recover them and bury them properly than let them float about for weeks. The Reverend Cunningham came out with us to bury those not identified. When we passed over the spot where the Titanic sank he held a short service in the Saloon, which I thought very nice of him.

I expected to see the poor creatures very disfigured, but they all look as calm as if they were asleep. Mack and I have had to keep six-hour watches all this trip so as to keep in touch with all ships and give them news. It is difficult to keep awake all night but I am getting used to it now.

May 2nd
Being again on watch it is now 3:00 A.M. I will write a little more. We have been

TITANIC BODY RECOVERY FACTS

★ Originally sixty *Titanic* victims buried in Halifax were unidentified. Over time, researchers have identified eighteen individuals, leaving forty-two buried under a number carved into a headstone.

★ On her maiden voyage, 2,228 people boarded *Titanic*; 705 survived the sinking; 1,523 perished at sea.

★ The Halifax-based cable ship *Mackay-Bennett* brought 190 *Titanic* victims to Halifax.

sailing about looking for bodies for the last four days and have only picked up seventeen. There has been a lot of wind and bad weather since the accident so the bodies are much scattered.

Some we picked up over 130 miles from the wreck as they go very fast when in the Gulf Stream. Very likely many will be washed up on the Irish Coast as they are all going East.

May 3rd

Just a few lines to let you know how things are going. I honestly hope I shall never have to come on another expedition like this as it is far from pleasant! The Doctor and I are sleeping in the middle of fourteen coffins (for the time being). They are all stacked around our quarters aft.

The Titanic must have been blown up when she sank as we have picked up pieces of the grand staircase and most of the wreckage is from below deck. It must have been an awful explosion too as some of the main deck planking four feet thick was all split and broken off short.

I guess the fellows on the Mackay-Bennett will get a bonus for this job and my word they deserve it after picking up over eight hundred [sic] bodies.

May 6th Halifax.

We arrived in port this morning. I hear the Mackay-Bennett fellows are to get a month's extra pay. I don't suppose we shall get a cent as we only got seventeen bodies.

They say there was tons of money on some of the bodies when they were picked up. Astor had $10,000, and another man had a bag of diamonds hung round his neck worth $250,000. Some of the jewels that went down in her were worth enough to buy a half dozen Minias. One woman's pearls alone were worth $450,000.

I am sorry to say that we have to go

out again in about two days up North, the same place we were when we heard about the Titanic. Etc. etc

Your loving son,
Frances Dyke

Two other ships were enlisted in the search for bodies but none found as many as the *Mackay-Bennett*, the "Death Ship."

The *Montmagny*, owned by the Canadian government's Department of Marine and Fisheries, left Sorel, Que., for Halifax on May 3. After picking up supplies and undertakers she searched around the Gulf of St. Lawrence for four days

The Canadian government owned vessel *Montmagny*, the third vessel to be sent to recover the *Titanic's* dead.

before finding the body of third-class passenger Harold Reynolds of Toronto, clinging to a life preserver. She would find three other bodies and bury one at sea before making port in Louisbourg, N.S., to send three bodies to Halifax by train.

The last of the 328 *Titanic* bodies pulled from the North Atlantic's icy grip was that of James McGrady, a saloon steward. He was picked up by *Algerine*, owned by Bowring Brothers of St. John's, Nfld., also hired by White Star. His body—the 209th to be taken to Halifax—arrived on June 11 aboard another Bowring ship. The following day he became the 150th and final *Titanic* victim to be laid to rest in Halifax.

MACKAY-BENNETT ARRIVES IN HALIFAX

"The Death Ship Will Arrive at Noon on April 28." The newspaper headline in the *Halifax Herald* said it all. *Mackay-Bennett*, a cable steamer hired by *Titanic's* owners the White Star Line, was steaming to Halifax with 190 bodies on board—nearly twice as many as she had coffins for when leaving port a week earlier.

The *Mackay-Bennett* usually berthed at what's now known as Karlsen's Wharf, just north of the Halifax Sheraton Hotel and Casino, but it was decided that the limited space on the bustling waterfront wouldn't be a suitable landing point for her macabre cargo. So *Mackay-Bennett* would travel another mile north into the harbour to use the Naval Dockyard North Coaling Wharf No.

Titanic bodies on deck of the Halifax ship *Mackay-Bennett*.

4. There a concrete wall would provide the security needed for the sombre task of unloading its human cargo.

The ship entered the harbour, her flag at half-mast, at about 9:30 A.M. on Tuesday, April 30—delayed by two days from the newspapers' predictions because of bad weather.

Stopping off Georges Island, just inside the harbour, she was boarded by the port doctor, the chief of police, and two detectives.

Captain Lardner and Canon Hind could be seen pacing the deck as she made her way to the dock, which is just north of where the Angus L. Macdonald Bridge stands today.

The seventy-five officers and crew lined the rails of the ship and on her stern were piled the one hundred coffins, filled with first class passengers who had been embalmed at sea. A large tarp covered the foredeck, covering rows of bodies for which there were no coffins. A mound of clothing was piled nearby. In the ice-filled hold there were still more dead.

Church bells rang, heads were lowered, and an eerie silence descended on

the dock as the three-hour job of unloading the corpses began.

"The first bodies taken ashore were those of the crew," reported the *Halifax*

Coffins lined the deck of the *Mackay-Bennett*.

Evening Mail. "These bodies had not been embalmed or even sewn up in canvas and presented such a gruesome sight that it would be almost impossible to picture." Crew of the *Mackay-Bennett* carried the bodies off the ship on stretchers. Others brought more bodies up from the hold, piling them in a heap of thirty or forty on the deck.

After *Titanic's* crew had left the ship, the second- and third-class passengers whose remains had been enclosed in canvas bags were removed by navy personnel. Finally, the first-class passengers—respectfully concealed in coffins— were carried off, already identified, embalmed, and ready for burial.

The prying eyes of the newspaper photographers were kept away from the dock by twenty sailors from the

Canadian cruiser *Niobe*, who acted as guards. A film crew on a tugboat that came too close had their vessel boarded and film seized.

Thirty horse-drawn hearses were hired to carry the dead a half-mile to the Mayflower Curling Rink, which was to become a makeshift morgue for the next ten days.

Churchgoers were urged during Sunday services two days earlier to stay away when the *Mackay-Bennett* docked. They apparently listened. There were only small groups on North Street as the hearses made their way toward Agricola Street, each one limited to ten coffins because of the steep hill

overlooking the harbour. Bystanders removed their hats, officers saluted, and silence descended on the tree-lined street as *Titanic's* dead moved across the city. Halifax was a city in shock and mourning. Much of the downtown was draped in black bunting, which surrounded photographs of *Titanic* in many of the business windows.

Once the bodies were inside the makeshift morgue, a crowd started to assemble on the street outside. Photographers took pictures of grief-stricken relatives as they waited to identify possible family members.

The *Halifax Morning Chronicle* reported on May 1, "Until a late hour last night, the temporary morgue at the Mayflower Curling Rink was the scene of much activity."

"From the time the bodies began to be

The hearse containing Astor's coffin. It would pass through the navy dockyard gate enroute to Snow's Funeral Home. Naval personnel and police control the many onlookers gathered to view the scene.

delivered there from the *Mackay-Bennett* until midnight the force of embalmers brought to the city by Snow and Co. were busily engaged preparing the bodies for burial."

"When one entered the morgue yesterday he was made to feel he was really entering the house of death."

A squad of policemen was on duty to ensure everything went smoothly but they needn't have bothered. The crowd of curious onlookers kept back from the building. Only those who came to Halifax to identify bodies of their family members were allowed inside the morgue.

For those who did get in, it was a curious sight. At the western end of the

Crew from the *Niobe* parade in front of the Dockyard c1911-12.

rink behind a partition, thirty-four benches had been set up for embalmers.

John Snow and Company Ltd., the largest funeral company in Nova Scotia, had been hired by White Star to prepare bodies for burial. John Snow knew it would be a demand unlike any he'd ever had before. So he had sent out a call for help to undertakers across Nova Scotia, Prince Edward Island, and New Brunswick.

Over forty responded and came to Halifax, including a woman from Saint John, N.B., whose job it would be to embalm *Titanic's* women and children.

For undertaker Frank Newell, who had come to Halifax from Yarmouth, there was a chilling shock awaiting. In the midst of preparing the bodies for burial he came across the remains of his uncle, first-class passenger Arthur W. Newell, a well-to-do banker from Lexington, Mass. The undertaker Newell had no idea his uncle had been aboard *Titanic*, and he fainted in shock.

Once the bodies were embalmed, they were brought out to the main rink where sixty-seven cubicles made of canvas had been set up with enough room for three coffins in each.

Friends and relatives were escorted into the cubicles to identify the victims. Family members could see bodies being moved to the cubicles from an observation area at the east end of the rink, which until days earlier had been used by cheering curling fans.

The temporary morgue set up in the Mayflower Curling Rink was quickly outfitted with partitioned cubicles, each designed to contain three bodies.

The *Evening Mail* reported that a small makeshift hospital was also set up and a nurse, Mrs. Nellie Remby, was on hand with plenty of smelling salts. "This was made all ready for the reception of those who had come for the purpose of identifying dear lost relatives and friends and who might well be expected to fall in a state of collapse when they recognized among the long rows of still and senseless forms those whom they had last seen in the full vigor of life and happiness."

The Intercolonial Railway opened a ticket office in the morgue so arrangements could be made to ship bodies home for burial. The cost of shipping a coffin in a baggage car was included in the price of a first-class rail ticket.

A coffin travelling express required two first-class tickets.

The rich and famous were spared the indignity of the Mayflower Curling Club and the observation room. The body of American John Jacob Astor, one of the richest men in the world, was carried from *Mackay-Bennett* to Snow's private mortuary on Argyle Street, a building which now houses a popular seafood restaurant, the Five Fishermen. Later when the *Minia*, another cable ship retrieving bodies, came back to Halifax on May 6, the body of Charles M. Hays, president of Grand Trunk Railway, went directly to the same funeral home.

A procession of hearses arrive at the Mayflower Curling Rink with *Titanic's* dead.

Astor's private rail car, the Oceanic, returned his body to the United States. Hays' remains were taken to the North Street railway station and put on a private rail car, Canada, for transport to Montreal, where he was buried.

Elsewhere in Halifax, an information bureau was established at the Halifax Hotel to help visitors who had come to the city in search of lost relatives find their way to the Mayflower Rink, the cemeteries and the churches where memorial services were held.

Upstairs at the Mayflower Rink the coroner's staff had set up a temporary office that was buzzing with activity, preparing a mountain of paperwork that was required to deal with the 209 bodies from *Titanic* that came to Halifax. In the end, fifty-nine of *Titanic's* victims were claimed and shipped to other locations

J.J. Astor's son, Vincent, leaving a telegraph office in Halifax.

for burial; 150 would remain in Halifax forever.

The Mayflower Rink, which today contains a store selling used army and navy gear, operated as a house of death for ten days in April and May of 1912.

On May 10, thirty-two bodies were transferred for burial at the Fairview Cemetery, leaving only four of *Titanic's* dead remaining at the Mayflower Rink. Two were scheduled for burial at Fairview the following day and another was claimed and prepared for the train trip out of Halifax. The other body was moved to Snow's mortuary on Argyle Street, to be joined by bodies recovered by the ships, *Montmagny* and *Algerine*.

Intercolonial Railway Station, North Street, Halifax.

It was time to close down the makeshift morgue. Two chests containing valuables worth between $50,000 and $75,000 were taken from the rink to the office of the provincial treasurer. At the end of the ordeal, representatives of the Nova Scotia government, the White Star Line, and the coroner's office completed their work, packed away their files and supplies and left the rink for the final time. Nevertheless, the part the rink played in one of the world's greatest marine disasters would never be forgotten.

The Halifax Hotel where an information bureau was established.

2

SERVICES FOR TITANIC'S DEAD

Halifax came out in full force to give *Titanic's* dead a proper burial in memorial services at the main churches throughout the city. "During the day, Halifax continued to be a city of mourning," declared the *Morning Chronicle*. "It lay under the shadow of a solemn hush."

The first of a host of services on Friday, May 3, two-and-a-half weeks after the sinking, was held at St. Mary's Cathedral.

Father John Foley, St. Mary's rector, conducted the morning service, along with Nova Scotia's Roman Catholic archbishop and six other priests. The large and ornate church, now known as St. Mary's Basilica, was filled to capacity and included officials from the White Star Line. Mourners overflowed onto the street.

Opposite page: The granite spire of St. Mary's Basilica on Spring Garden Road, Halifax.

The interior of St. Mary's as it appeared around the time of the *Titanic* disaster. It was here that funerals for Roman Catholic victims were held on May 3, 1912.

Four unidentified females from the wreck—one was later identified as third-class passenger Margaret Rice—were placed on a catafalque in the sanctuary for the service. They were buried later that day at Mount Olivet Cemetery.

On the same day, a funeral for fifty *Titanic* victims, who were mostly unidentified, was held at Brunswick Street Methodist Church (destroyed by fire in 1979) under the direc-

A view of Brunswick Street Methodist Church in Halifax's North End c1912.

tion of the Halifax Evangelical Alliance. Inside the church, purple and black bunting was draped throughout. Large bunches of pink and white carnations surrounded the pulpit. The flowers were a gift of Mrs. Hugh R. Rood, wife of a first-class passenger who drowned aboard *Titanic*. She also paid for flowers for the unidentified dead at the Mayflower Curling Rink.

In attendance at Brunswick Street Methodist Church was the lieutenant-governor of Nova Scotia, the officers of

The interior of Brunswick Street Methodist Church decorated for Easter services c1911-12.

the Canadian cruiser *Niobe*, whose sailors acted as guards when the Death Ship, *Mackay-Bennett*, unloaded her human cargo. The Very Rev. Dean Crawford read Psalm 90—"Lord thou hast been our dwelling place...." The Rev. Clarence MacKinnon of the Presbyterian College at Pine Hill delivered the sermon.

The Royal Canadian Regiment band played the hymns, "Forever With the Lord," "Hymn for the Survivors of the *Titanic*" especially written by Hall Caine and the sombre melody reputedly played by *Titanic's* band as she slipped out of sight, "Nearer My God To Thee."

THE GUARDIAN ANGEL OF THE SEA PAYS TRIBUTE TO THE MARTYRED HEROES

An illustration that appeared in one of the many books published shortly after the *Titanic* disaster.

In the afternoon, a crowd of seven hundred moved to Fairview Cemetery where burial took place. "These are the unidentified, but they are unforgotten and in Halifax their graves will be kept forever green," said the Rev. MacKinnon.

"We can never tell what mother's kiss soothed their infant sorrows nor in what tongue the cradle song hushed them to slumber."

The coffins were buried in long trenches. Each grave would eventually have a headstone on which was carved the number which signified the order in which it was recovered from its watery grave.

One man buried in Fairview that day was later exhumed and reburied in

Mount Olivet Cemetery after he was identified and determined to be a Roman Catholic. First-class passenger Serrando Ovies y Rodrigues was moved on May 15—nearly two weeks later.

Niobe Crew c 1911-12.

Also buried on that Friday, May 3, were nine bodies in the Jewish Baron de Hirsch Cemetery, immediately adjacent to Fairview Cemetery.

All of Halifax was affected by the *Titanic* tragedy. Church bells had been ringing for the dead since earlier in the week when the steamer *Mackay-Bennett* brought 190 bodies ashore.

"Mother earth took the first quota of *Titanic* victims to her bosom yesterday," said the *Chronicle*, describing the service at Fairview Cemetery.

"As the solemn service proceeded the emotion of the crowd showed itself. Women wept, while the tears were seen running down the cheeks of men, some of whom had faced death in the hour of battle."

Engineering Officers, *Niobe*, 1911.

Canada's first naval ship *Niobe*.

The newspaper reported that the band played "Nearer My God To Thee" again at the cemetery, where a kilted band of bagpipers joined in.

"It was not alone that the band of the Royal Canadians was on duty at Fairview

Views of St. Paul's Church and card for the *Titanic* memorial service.

Cemetery, swelling out, as the bodies were lowered into the ground, the same pathetic strain that rang in the ears of the dead as the waves closed over their heads."

Another service was held at St. Paul's Anglican church for Halifax millionaire George Wright, whose body was never recovered.

Memorial Service

Victims of S. S. "Titanic,"

Lost off Newfoundland Banks, on the night of April 14th, 1912, with more than a thousand five hundred passengers.

At St. Paul's Church,

HALIFAX, N. S.

Sunday, April 21st. 1912.

St. Paul's Church, Halifax

The congregation of St. George's Anglican church, prayed for a mysterious two-year-old boy, who became known as the Unknown Child of *Titanic*.

The Georgian interior of St. George's Church.

Prayers for Gosta Paulson, Titanic's Unknown Child, were said at St. George's.

STORY OF STANLEY FOX

There are many mysterious events surrounding *Titanic's* sinking, but none perhaps more bizarre than the saga of Stanley H. Fox.

Fox, a thirty-eight-year-old travelling salesman from Rochester, N.Y., died aboard *Titanic* returning from a business trip to England. His body was recovered by the cable steamer *Mackay-Bennett* and taken to Halifax. His death certificate was issued by coroner W. D. Flinn and his burial permit by John Barnstead, the deputy registrar of deaths. His story took a strange twist when a woman named Lydia Fox, who said she was Fox's sister-in-law, arrived in Halifax by train with an unidentified man and claimed the body on behalf of Fox's widow, Cora.

The widow, according to the *Evening Mail* newspaper, was "ill at home, pros-trated by the news that her husband was one of the *Titanic* victims."

Assuming Lydia Fox had legitimate claim to the body, the coroner and White Star Line agents directed Fox's body to the train station and prepared to release his personal effects, about seventy dollars in cash and two watches.

But an hour before the train left, a telegram arrived from Cora Fox, the widow, that read: "Do not deliver body of Stanley H. Fox to anyone representing themselves as Mrs. Morton R. Fox or Lyda [sic] Fox. But embalm and send by express to wife. Wire reply. Mrs. Stanley H. Fox."

Lydia Fox was upset by the telegram and couldn't explain why it had been sent, although she was apparently out-raged by the suspicions it aroused. The authorities were also confused. They allowed the body to be released with Lydia Fox but kept Stanley Fox's watches and his money.

Lydia Fox left Halifax with Stanley Fox's body, en route to New York. The train was about half an hour out of Halifax when another telegram arrived from Rochester: "Mrs. Lydia Fox, care (of) Snow Undertaker—Mayflower Rink-Halifax," wrote Cora Fox, Stanley's widow. "I give you no right to claim body or effects. Cora."

That was enough for the authorities. Fearing insurance fraud, they ordered the train stopped in Truro, about one hundred kilometres north of Halifax. The body was removed, unknown to Lydia Fox, who continued the trip to Rochester without knowing that Stanley Fox was no longer aboard.

A couple of days later, the mayor of Rochester intervened and sent a telegram to Halifax, directing that the body, which had been kept in Truro, be sent on to Cora Fox.

The authorities in Halifax apparently never determined why Lydia Fox wanted Stanley Fox's body, reported the *Evening News*, which delighted in the scandal. "They are congratulating themselves, however, that the personal effects—seventy dollars and two watches—were not handed to her. The widow is known to have been acquainted with the claimant, but declined to let her have anything to do either with the body or the effects." Nothing was ever heard of again from Lydia or the man who accompanied her in Halifax.

The Fox story telegrams.

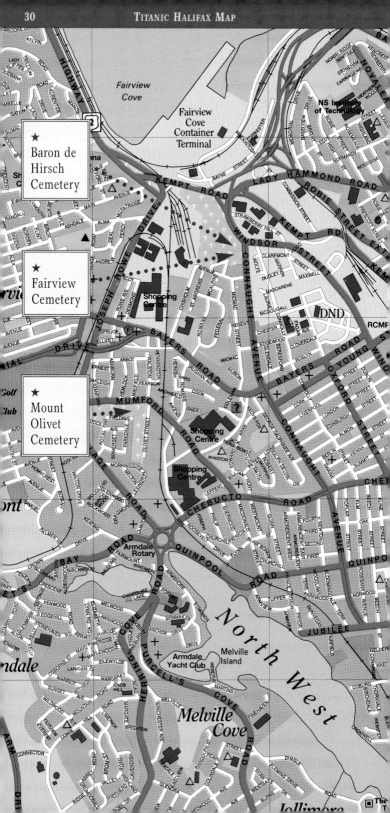

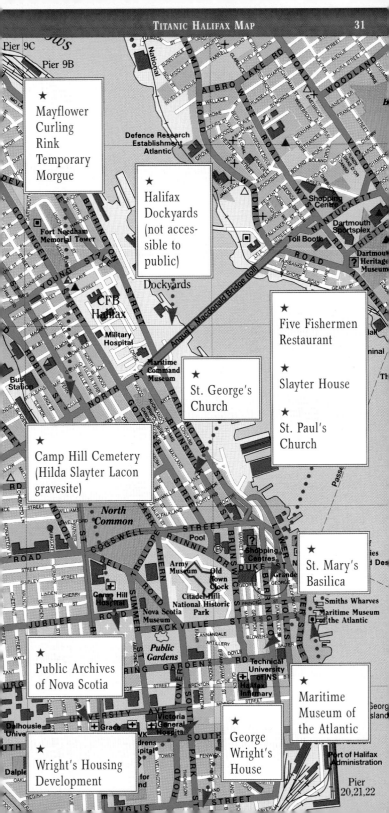

★ Mayflower Curling Rink Temporary Morgue

★ Halifax Dockyards (not accessible to public)

★ Five Fishermen Restaurant

★ Slayter House

★ St. George's Church

★ St. Paul's Church

★ Camp Hill Cemetery (Hilda Slayter Lacon gravesite)

★ St. Mary's Basilica

★ Public Archives of Nova Scotia

★ Maritime Museum of the Atlantic

★ George Wright's House

★ Wright's Housing Development

Halifax Titanic Sites

Titanic's Cemeteries

The most enduring legacy in Halifax of *Titanic's* sinking is found in three cemeteries in the city where 150 victims are a reminder of the most famous maritime disaster in history. These graves contain the bodies that were either unidentified, unclaimed, or requested by relatives to be buried in Halifax.

The world's largest group of *Titanic* graves is in the non-denominational Fairview Cemetery. There, 121 graves are marked by plain black granite gravestones that wind their way up a gentle hillside in the curved shape of a ship's hull. The sloping front of the grave markers all carry the same date: April 15, 1912. Some have names. Some do not. However, all have numbers corresponding to the order in which they were recovered.

It's a similar but smaller scene in the neighbouring Baron de Hirsch Jewish Cemetery-where there are ten *Titanic* victims—and a few blocks away at Mount Olivet Roman Catholic cemetery, where there are nineteen graves from *Titanic*.

Today, visitors are paying their respects to *Titanic's* memory by visiting these cemeteries, proving predictions made during the 1912 grave-side ceremonies that the victims would never be forgotten.

Top inset: Baron de Hirsch Jewish Cemetery.

Background and centre inset: The graves of *Titanic* victims in the Fairview Cemetery are laid out in the shape of a ship's bow.

Inset bottom: Mount Olivet Cemetery.

FAIRVIEW CEMETERY

Directions: Fairview Cemetery is in the North End of Halifax, near the intersection

of Windsor Street and Kempt Road, overlooking the Bedford Basin. The entrance to the cemetery is on Windsor Street across from a Ford dealership. The cemetery is marked with a sign containing a reference to Titanic graves.

From downtown Halifax, travel north on Barrington Street under the A. Murray MacKay Bridge and straight through the intersection of Kempt Road and Windsor Street. Fairview Cemetery is on the right, just past the intersection.

It's in the Fairview Cemetery that some of the most gripping stories of *Titanic's* link to Halifax can be found. And the graveyard tells a story of its own.

One of the first things people notice at Fairview is that

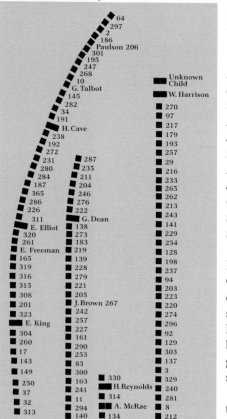

64
297
2
186
Paulson 206
301
195
247
268
10
G. Talbot
145
282
34
191
H. Cave
238
192
272
231
280
284
187
365
286
226
311
E. Elliot
320
261
E. Freeman
165
319
316
315
308
201
323
E. King
304
260
17
143
149
250
37
32
313

287
235
211
204
246
276
222
G. Dean 138
273
183
219
139
228
279
221
205
J. Brown 267
242
257
227
161
290
253
83
300
163
241
11
294
140

330
H. Reynolds
314
A. McRae
134

Unknown Child
W. Harrison
270
97
217
179
193
257
29
216
233
265
262
213
243
141
229
254
128
198
237
94
203
223
220
274
296
92
129
303
137
3
329
240
281
8
212

each grave, whether identified by name or not, bears a number under the identical date of death: April 15, 1912.

The number carved into the native Nova Scotia granite represents the order in which bodies were hauled from the icy North Atlantic.

Another unique feature of Fairview's *Titanic* graves is that they're laid out not in straight lines or perfect rows but are purposely bowed and bent in the shape of a ship's hull.

There's a gap left between graves on the starboard—or right-hand side—of the tidy rows, representing where *Titanic* struck the iceberg that ripped a hole in her inch-thick hull.

What the gravediggers of Halifax in 1912 could not have known was that by positioning their monuments to face north-east, they were preparing a tribute more fitting then they could have imagined.

When *Titanic's* wreck was located decades later on the ocean floor, it was discovered that her bow had come to rest in the exact same direction—facing the north-east like the *Titanic* graves of Halifax.

Buried at Fairview is James Dawson, an Irish coal trimmer who has become con-fused with a fictional character, Jack Dawson, played by actor Leonardo DiCaprio in the movie, "Titanic."

Also buried at Fairview is Alma Paulson, a Swedish emigrant who played the harmonica to calm her four children on the deck of the sinking liner. Her youngest child, two-year-old Gosta, was later found to be the Unknown Child of *Titanic* who touched the heart of the city.

Opposite page: A visitor views the grave of A. McRae with its imposing celtic cross.

Titanic Purser's Clerk, Ernest W. King is buried at Fairview Cemetery.

Fairview Cemetery.

And there are heroes, such as William Denton Cox, a *Titanic* steward from Southampton, England. Not much is known about Cox's past, but it is known that he led groups of third-class passengers up to the top deck as *Titanic* was sinking. He was aided by third-class steward John Edward Hart and Albert Victory Pearcey, a pantryman. Cox was the only one of the three to die in the sinking. Hart and Pearcey climbed into lifeboats and were saved.

One of many graves identified with a number.

ALMA PAULSON

Behind every *Titanic* grave in Halifax is a tragic story. Perhaps none is as heart-breaking as that of twenty-nine year-old Swedish emigrant Alma Paulson and how she came to be reunited in death with her two-year-old son who was, for a time, the Unknown Child of *Titanic*.

Alma Paulson.

Paulson—whose headstone is on the left-hand side of the Fairview graves, near what would be the bow of the ship-boarded the *Titanic* with her four children en route to join her husband, Nils in Chicago.

Nils had worked hard to send home money for his family's journey. But since money was tight for the Paulson family in Bjuv, Sweden, Alma and her children were third-class passengers. They were below decks when *Titanic* rammed into the iceberg on April 14, 1912. Tragically, they stayed there until the last of the lifeboats were launched.

Eventually, Paulson and her children made it onto the deck. Accounts from that terrible night say she bundled them up against the cold and bravely played a harmonica to keep them calm. One can only imagine the horrific picture of Alma huddled with her four children as

Titanic's bow began to sink into the black Atlantic.

Paulson's body was pulled from the icy water several days later by the Halifax-based ship *Mackay-Bennett*, hired for the job of body recovery by the White Star Line, owners of *Titanic*. She was easily identified by her ticket, No. 340009, that was found in her purse, along with a letter from her husband and the harmonica.

Not so easily identified, however, was her two-year-old son, Gosta.

His was the fourth body recovered following the disaster by *Mackay-Bennett*, just after daylight on Sunday, April 21. The little blond-haired boy was dressed in a grey coat with fur on collar and cuffs, a brown serge frock and petticoat when he was found by the *Mackay-Bennett* crew.

Newspapers picked up on the sad story when there was no way to identify the only child recovered after the sinking: "Over in one corner of the morgue lay the bodies of the women recovered from the sea and in midst is the body of the little two-year-old boy," says a heart-wrenching account in the May 3 edition of the *Halifax Morning Chronicle*.

"The body of the little baby has been placed in a little white casket upon a bed of flowers."

The following day a moving service was conducted at St. George's Anglican Church, (the Round Church), for the mysterious boy. Canon Kenneth O. Hind, who had been on the steamer *Mackay-Bennett* when the boy's body was found, officiated at the service. Offers to sponsor the funeral had come in from around the city and beyond, but at the request of Captain F. H. Lardner of the *Mackay-*

The grave stone of Alma Paulson, mother of the "Unknown Child."

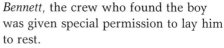

Gosta Paulson.

The grave of Gosta Paulson. The special headstone was bought by crewmembers of the *Mackay-Bennett*.

Bennett, the crew who found the boy was given special permission to lay him to rest.

At the funeral, the seventy-five officers and crew of *Mackay-Bennett* were on hand, as well as many others in the city who had been deeply touched by the child's fate.

At the conclusion of the service, the boy's coffin was covered with flowers and carried from the church by six sailors from the *Mackay-Bennett*. The crew accompanied the horse-drawn hearse to Fairview Cemetery. On the previous day there had been fifty unknown *Titanic* victims laid to rest there. On this day, it was the death of one child that was being marked.

The crew had a headstone erected that was larger than the simple granite markers on the other graves. On it appears the following inscription: "Erected to the memory of an Unknown Child whose remains were recovered after the disaster of the *Titanic*, April 15, 1912."

The sailors had no way of knowing that the child who had touched the hearts of so many was Gosta Paulson. And they did not know that his final resting place was just feet away from the grave of his mother, Alma Paulson.

Paulson's other children were never found.

J. DAWSON

One of the most visited and decorated of the *Titanic* graves in Halifax these days is that of J. Dawson. School girls and other visitors shower the simple marker at the Fairview Cemetery with single red roses, bouquets of flowers, candy, heart-felt poems and even ticket stubs from the movie "Titanic."

They don't know—or perhaps don't want to know—that this is not Jack Dawson, the role made famous by actor Leonardo DiCaprio in the blockbuster movie.

In the movie, the character Jack Dawson died in the tragedy, but that's the only similarity with the real J. Dawson. The fictionalized character played by DiCaprio was a free-spirited American artist who fell in

love with first-class passenger, Rose DeWitt Bukater, played by actor Kate Winslet. This Dawson won a third-class ticket on *Titanic* in a poker game and stumbled into a class-crossing romance that was all but impossible in the rigid social system of 1912.

Stokers and trimmers were called the "black gang."

Titanic cross section showing the decks—the lower two containing the boilers and coal bunkers where Dawson worked as a "trimmer."

(In fact, on the real *Titanic*, some third class passengers were shot while trying to get into *Titanic* lifeboats ahead of their more well-to-do shipmates.)

The real J. Dawson who lies buried at Fairview Cemetery was James Dawson, a twenty-three-year-old native of Dublin, Ireland. The sandy-haired, mustachioed Dawson was down on his luck when he left home in search of work. No doubt

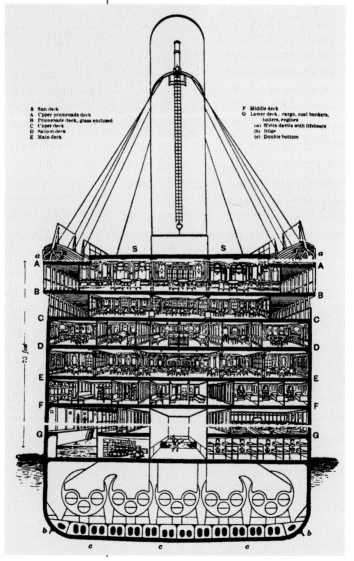

8 Sun deck
A Upper promenade deck
B Promenade deck, glass enclosed
C Upper deck
D Saloon deck
E Main deck

F Middle deck
G Lower deck: cargo, coal bunkers,
   boilers, engines
   (a) Welin davits with lifeboats
   (b) Bilge
   (c) Double bottom

he thought his luck improved when he landed in Southampton—*Titanic's* home port.

Unemployment was high in the south of England at the time. But *Titanic* was the world's biggest ship and needed an equally large crew—885 in all. Dawson was hired on as one of about twenty coal trimmers, one of the lowliest jobs on the ship. He worked in what would be an unbearable conditions by today's standards—hot, smoky, filthy, and dangerous.

His job was to move the coal from the storage area (where a small, inconsequential fire had broken out before *Titanic* left port), to the stokers who manned the furnaces, and also kept the weight of the coal balanced on the ship; thus the name "trimmer."

Titanic's trimmers and stokers fed the massive coal-fired furnaces that boiled water to drive the great steam engines. The engines could move *Titanic's* massive hulk at impressive speeds such as the twenty-five miles (forty kilometres) an hour she was travelling when she hit the iceberg.

Although Dawson's world on *Titanic* was a seething inferno, it was no doubt better than the fate that awaited him and many others of the below-deck crews who perished in the icy waters of the North Atlantic.

Dawson's body was found intact by the cable steamer, *Mackay-Bennett* over a week after the sinking. He was dressed in the coal-stained denim coat and pants that marked his place on the ship.

Now his place is marked by a stone of Nova Scotia granite and honoured by many who visit Fairview Cemetery.

Plan of lower deck of the *Titanic*.

ERNEST FREEMAN AND BRUCE ISMAY

There are several graves at the Fairview Cemetery which are larger and more prominent than the simple, plain stones marking most of *Titanic's* dead. Among them is the grave of Ernest Edward Samuel Freeman. He was the fifty-year-old secretary to White Star Line chairman Bruce Ismay, who was accused of cowardice for surviving the tragedy.

Ernest Freeman.

On Freeman's granite grave marker, there is an inscription that reads: "He remained at his post of duty, seeking to save others regardless of his own life and went down with the ship." Another inscription at the base of the stone reads: "Erected by Mr. J. Bruce Ismay. To commemorate a long and faithful service."

Some say it was guilt that motivated Ismay, often described as a cold and selfish man, to honour his secretary in death. Aside from erecting the memorial to his former employee, Ismay made arrangements for a personal pension to be paid to Ernest Freeman's family back in Southampton, *Titanic's* home port.

Freeman's grave marker was erected by White Star Line chairman Bruce Ismay.

Ismay, who made a habit of sailing on the maiden voyage of all White Star ships, was the subject of immediate criticism following the disaster. He was branded a coward for surviving and accused of ordering *Titanic* to travel at unsafe speeds as part of an ill-fated publicity stunt to arrive in New York a day ahead of schedule. The accusations were scandalous and far-fetched. He was accused of dressing in women's clothes, jumping into the first lifeboat, and trying to suppress news of the disaster to collect more insurance money. Ismay mounted a vigorous defence. A U.S. Senate hearing was held in the ballroom of the Waldorf-Astoria Hotel in New York within days of the sinking. Following is an exchange between Ismay and Senator William Alden Smith of Michigan taken from the hearing:

Smith: What were the circumstances of your departure from the ship?

Ismay: The boat was there. There were a certain number of men in the boat and the officer called out, asking if there were any more women, and there was no response and there were no passengers left on the deck.

Smith: There were no passengers on the deck?

White Star Line chairman Bruce Ismay.

Ismay: No sir, and as the boat was in the act of being lowered away, I got into it.

Smith: At that time, the *Titanic* was sinking?

Ismay: She was sinking.

Ismay's testimony fell on deaf ears. Although his story was collaborated by another survivor, he was branded a coward and an accomplice to the sinking.

The investigation condemned both Ismay and White Star for *Titanic's* excessive speed in dangerous seas and for having too few lifeboats on board. However, neither was ever formally charged.

United States Congressional Hearings.

A cartoon criticizing Ismay.

A British inquiry later cleared Ismay of any wrongdoing, but the damage was done. Ismay eventually resigned his position with the White Star Line, the company his father had founded, and lived out the twenty-five years following *Titanic's* sinking as a relative recluse in Ireland.

TITANIC BAND

At least two members of *Titanic's* famous orchestra are buried in Halifax cemeteries—first violinist John Law (Jock) Hume who is buried in Fairview Cemetery and bass violinist John Frederick Preston Clarke who is buried in Mount Olivet.

The band is well known for playing while *Titanic* was sinking—both to keep panic to a minimum and to strengthen the spirits of those unable to find a place on a lifeboat. The eight band members, who all died, dutifully kept to their post—a makeshift stage on A Deck near the lifeboats.

There has been much dispute about whether the band played the sombre hymn, "Nearer My God to Thee" as the ship sank out of sight. However, there is no question that the band members were heroes.

In their honour, the same sad strains of "Nearer My God to Thee" were played by a military band at the May 3, 1912, ceremony at Fairview Cemetery, which holds Hume's grave.

The Rev. Clarence MacKinnon paid tribute to all of the musicians at Hume's burial. "Perhaps no incident in modern times has more deeply stirred the admiration of the world than the spectacle of those self-disciplined men, picking up their instruments in such a tragic

The body of Wallace Henry Hartley, bandleader was recovered and sent via Boston to England for burial.

moment and playing sprightly melodies to allay the anxiety of the passengers and permit the officers of the ship to fill the boats without panic. Until at length the tilting deck warned them that their task was done and changing to a tune now double consecrated, passed forever nearer our God to Thee, nearer to Thee."

Less is known about John Clarke, the other *Titanic* musician buried in Halifax's Mount Olivet Roman Catholic Cemetery. Clarke was from Liverpool and was wearing the same band uniform when his body was found by the cable ship *Mackay-Bennett*. The only other *Titanic* musician whose remains were recovered was Wallace Henry Hartley, the orchestra leader. His body was transferred from Halifax to Boston and then on to Liverpool and finally to his boyhood hometown of Colne in Lancashire, England.

The body of band member Jock Law Hume was interred in Fairview Cemetery, May 8, 1912.

JOCK HUME

Jock Hume was a curly-haired, baby-faced twenty-eight-year-old who came from Dumfries, Scotland. Like the other members of the band, he died in his band uniform, with green facing and vest. It was that uniform that helped with his identification. A photograph of his body was taken and sent to the offices of the White Star Line in Southampton.

"We expected this body to be identified as the uniform and effects indicated that it was that of one of the bandsmen," said a July 16, 1912, letter to provincial officials from White Star's office. "The parents of Mr. Hume have asked for the effects, which are of trifling value, and we hope that you may see your way to let us have them, which we will greatly appreciate."

The Liverpool company that hired the band for *Titanic* wrote callously to Hume's father on April 30, 1912—just two weeks after the sinking. They insisted Hume's father pay for his son's band uniform.

Cover of White Star Line Music Book.

Titanic musicians took a salary cut before signing on the voyage. They were employees of a Liverpool company, C. W. and F. N. Black, which supplied orchestras to the steamship companies. Before 1912, they were paid six pounds and ten shillings a month plus a monthly uniform. The pay was cut to four pounds a month and the uniform allowance was ended.

On April 30, 1912, Jock Hume's father received this short and unwelcome note from Blacks:

Dear Sir:
We shall be obliged if you will remit us the sum of 5s. 4d., which is owing to us as per enclosed statement. We shall also be obliged if you will settle the enclosed uniform account.

Yours faithfully,
C. W. & F. N. Black

The company wanted two shillings for lapel insignias shaped like lyres and one shilling for sewing buttons with the White Star logo on Jock Hume's uniform jacket for a bill of fourteen shillings, seven pence.

BARON DE HIRSCH CEMETERY

Directions: Baron de Hirsch Cemetery is on the corner of Connaught Avenue and Windsor Street and is adjacent to Fairview Cemetery. The entrance to the cemetery is on Connaught Avenue and is not normally open to the public.

There are just ten *Titanic* graves in the Baron de Hirsch Jewish Cemetery, which borders the Fairview Cemetery on the south.

■ 289	■ 278
■ 291	■ 214
■ 136	■ 114 Wormald
■ 248	■ 264
■ 7	■ 15 Navratil

They all bear the familiar numerical inscription with the identical date of death: April 15, 1912. The graves are orderly, in neat and formal rows overlooking a treed ravine among the Stars of David on the other nearby stones. All but two of the graves are nameless, their identities remaining a mystery.

Of the two identified graves, one should not have been buried in the Jewish cemetery at all. It was a bizarre case of mistaken identity! Fugitive Michel Navratil had abducted his two

The *Titanic* graves in the Baron de Hirsch Cemetery. All but one of the 10 buried here are of Jewish descent.

sons from his estranged wife and had given the false name of Louis M. Hoffman, leading officials to believe he was Jewish.

THE MISSING BODIES

This was not the only case of mistaken identity. For a few hours the local rabbi, Jacob Walter, had secured what he believed were ten more Jewish victims for the cemetery by taking them from among a group of bodies awaiting burial in the neighbouring Fairview Cemetery.

Rabbi Jacob Walter (centre) and two workmen pose after placing gravestones at the Baron de Hirsch Jewish Cemetery.

On Friday, May 3, about seven hundred mourners had crowded into the Fairview Cemetery for a grave-side service for fifty *Titanic* victims, mostly unidentified. The Royal Canadian Regiment band was playing. Kilted bagpipers were assembled.

Suddenly, officials noticed that there were only forty bodies laid out for burial instead of the fifty for whom burial papers had been prepared.

It was later revealed that Rabbi Walter and leading members of Halifax's Jewish community were responsible

for the missing bodies.

"Something of a sensation was created at Fairview Cemetery yesterday when the funeral services began over the bodies of the unidentified *Titanic* dead," the *Halifax Evening News* reported the following day.

It turned out that while funeral services for the fifty unidentified victims were under way across the city at Brunswick Street Methodist Church, Rabbi Walter and his helpers had been examining bodies awaiting burial in Fairview. The rabbi felt that he hadn't been given enough time for a thorough investigation the previous night while the bodies were still at the makeshift morgue, the Mayflower Curling Rink.

The newspaper picked up the story: "The rabbi therefore returned to the Fairview Cemetery, opened the coffins awaiting internment, satisfied himself that ten of them contained bodies of Hebrews and then directed the undertaker's team to take them to the Jewish cemetery. He acted thus promptly he says because if he had waited, the burial would have taken place and he would have been too late."

Rabbi Walter had identified nine Jewish victims on his brief inspection at the morgue the previous night. After a more thorough inspection at Fairview, he had identified and claimed a total of nineteen Jewish bodies. He ordered extra gravediggers to complete the job before sundown Friday, which marked the beginning of the Jewish Sabbath, after which work would not be allowed.

However, when the grave-side service at Fairview Cemetery was finished, the authorities who noticed the discrepancy in the number of coffins, marched up over the hill to Baron de Hirsch Cemetery to speak to the rabbi.

They ordered the digging to stop. The original nine Jewish victims were buried as planned and the ten bodies in dispute were placed in the receiving vault at Baron de Hirsch. Delicate negotiations commenced.

When Rabbi Walter initially inspected the 190 bodies slated for burial in Halifax, he identified 44 that he believed to be Jewish. Newspaper accounts don't explain how that number was reduced to nine. However, it is known that one of the men he claimed for Baron de Hirsch was later identified as an Irishman named Galway. Others were identified by non-Jewish relatives, and later four were found to be Roman Catholics so were sent to Mount Olivet Cemetery for burial.

The ten coffins removed from Fairview Cemetery by the rabbi were eventually returned to the morgue at the curling rink on orders from provincial authorities and the White Star Line, owners of *Titanic*. They were later buried at Fairview, where they remain today.

MICHEL NAVRATIL

In Halifax's Baron de Hirsch Jewish Cemetery is the grave of Roman Catholic Michel Navratil and also the answer to the mystery of the Orphans of the *Titanic*.

The tortuous tale begins in France where Navratil moved from his native Slovakia in 1902. He met and married a young Italian woman, Marcelle Carretto, and had two sons, Michel and Edmond.

By 1912, the year of *Titanic's* voyage, his tailor's business was foundering, and the marriage had broken up over Michel's suspicions that his wife was having an affair.

A Catholic, Michel Navratil is buried in the Jewish Baron de Hirsch Cemetery.

Grave of
Michel Navatril.

The lifeboat
Collapsible D
containing the
two Navatril
children
approaches the
Carpathia.

The boys lived with their mother and often visited their father. After such a visit on Easter weekend, Navratil and the boys vanished. No one knew they were on their way to a new life in America—aboard *Titanic*.

Navratil made a quick stop in Monte Carlo and then sailed for England where he purchased second-class tickets aboard *Titanic* under the assumed name of Louis Hoffman. The boys were also given false identities—Loto and Louis.

Navratil, a dark-haired man with a thick moustache, kept to himself on board ship and rarely let the boys out of his sight. His cover story was that Mrs. Hoffman was dead. He seemed to be prepared for the worst as he carried a loaded revolver with him at all times.

After *Titanic* hit the iceberg, Navratil and another passenger dressed the boys and went above deck to find a lifeboat.

"My father entered our cabin where we were sleeping," the older son, Michel Jr., recalled years later. "He dressed me very warmly and took me in his arms. A stranger did the same for my brother. When I think of it now, I am very moved. They knew they were going to die."

The two men rushed the boys to the lifeboat Collapsible D, but an officer had ordered crew members to surround it with locked arms to ensure that only women and children got on board.

Navratil handed the boys through the human chain and stepped back.

Michel Jr., who was three years old at the time, recalled his father's final words. "My child, when your mother comes for you, as she surely will, tell her that I loved her dearly and still do. Tell her I expected her to follow us so that we might all live happily together in the peace and freedom of the New World."

The boys and the other survivors in Collapsible D were picked up by the Cunard liner *Carpathia* and taken to New York. But because they spoke no English and nothing could be learned

The identity of the two *Titanic* orphans, Edmond and Michel Jr., remained unknown for several weeks until their mother identified them from newspaper photographs.

about the mysterious Louis Hoffman, their identities remained a mystery. The mystery was solved when their frantic mother read the story of the Orphans of

The *"Titanic Orphans"* reunited with their mother.

Titanic in the newspapers and saw their picture. The White Star Line brought her to America where she was reunited with her sons on May 16, before returning to France on the liner *Oceanic*.

Michel Navratil was last seen handing his children through the circle of crew around Collapsible D. His body was among the first to be found by the Halifax-based cable ship *Mackay-Bennett* on April 21. Dressed in a grey overcoat and brown suit there was little to identify him other than his second-class ticket, No. 230080, purchased in the name of Louis Hoffman. In his pockets were a gold watch and chain, some money, a pipe, a London hotel receipt, and his loaded revolver.

Navratil's widow, Marcelle.

Because of the name Navratil had chosen as an alias, he was buried in Halifax's Baron de Hirsch Cemetery with nine others from *Titanic*. When the secret of the Orphans of *Titanic* was revealed, his real name was etched into the granite grave marker, where it remains today.

Michel Navratil Jr. came to Halifax on Aug. 27, 1996, at eighty-eight years of age to visit his father's grave for the first time. While a Roman Catholic priest blessed the site, Navratil clasped his hands in prayer and gazed smiling at the grave marker bearing his father's name. With sparkling eyes, he told the priest he could hear the music his father loved and felt the presence of an angel.

MOUNT OLIVET CEMETERY

Directions: Mount Olivet Cemetery is on Mumford Road near Dutch Village Road. To get there from downtown Halifax, go west on Cogswell Street to Quinpool Road and then right onto Connaught Avenue. Turn left on Chebucto Road and then right on Mumford Road. Pass between two shopping centres and over railway tracks. The entrance to the cemetery is on the left.

The *Titanic* graves at Mount Olivet Cemetery.

Like all of the *Titanic* graves in Halifax, those at the Mount Olivet Roman Catholic cemetery share the same stark, simple granite headstones as those of the Jewish and Protestant victims. There are nineteen of *Titanic's* dead at Mount Olivet.

The Mount Olivet cemetery contains fewer *Titanic* graves than the Fairview Cemetery but all the grave sites deserve respect and consideration. A sign marks the grave site and flowers left by Halifax residents and other visitors grace many of the graves.

	298
328	302
189	244
277	215
306	5
188	202
79	288
312	210
266	13
196	12

Many of the victims buried at Mount Olivet are not named and are known only by the number carved into the Nova Scotia black granite that signifies the order in which they were pulled from the North Atlantic. All have the mark common to every *Titanic* victim buried in Halifax: April 15, 1912, the date that *Titanic* sank seven hundred miles east of Halifax, after colliding with an iceberg just before midnight on April 14.

JOHN CLARKE

One of *Titanic's* band members, John Clarke, is buried here; his grave is marked with his name and the number 202. Clarke was from Liverpool and went by the popular nickname "Nobby" used for sailors named Clarke in the British navy and merchant marine. When Clarke's body was discovered he was wearing a green-fronted bandsmen's uniform. The band is remembered for its heroism that fateful night, when it stoically continued to play on Titanic's deck until the last passengers had left the ship and the waves engulfed them.

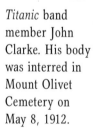

Titanic band member John Clarke. His body was interred in Mount Olivet Cemetery on May 8, 1912.

SERRANDO OVIES Y RODRIGUES

Also buried at Mount Olivet is the body of Serrando Ovies y Rodrigues, the only *Titanic* victim to be exhumed. Ovies y Rodrigues, which is also spelled Rodriguez, was buried here on May 15, 1912. He was a first-class passenger initially laid to rest in the Fairview Cemetery in Halifax's North End. When he was later identified and determined to be Roman Catholic he was exhumed and reburied in Catholic consecrated ground.

TITANIC SINKING FACTS

★ *Titanic* sank in 12,500 ft. of water, almost three miles down. The wreck lies seven hundred miles east of Halifax.

★ *Titanic* broke into two pieces when she sank—the bow section, and the stern section.

★ At 10:35 P.M. Newfoundland time on April 14, 1912, *Titanic* sent a message to a station in Cape Race, Nfld., that she had "struck iceberg."

★ My God, Gray, the *Titanic* has struck a berg," were the words of Newfoundland radio operator Jack Goodwin spoken to fellow operator Walter Gray when the first S O S from *Titanic* was received.

★ At 11:36 P.M. Newfoundland time on April 14, 1912, *Titanic* again signalled to Cape Race, Nfld. "We are putting women off in boats."

★ At 12:27 A.M. Newfoundland time on April 15, 1912, the Cape Race, Nfld., station received *Titanic's* last blurred wireless signal.

OTHER HALIFAX
TITANIC SITES

4

HALIFAX
WATERFRONT

Halifax contains many sites and places touched by the *Titanic* tragedy. If you stand on the boardwalks on the Halifax waterfront and look out at the harbour, you can well imagine what it must have been like in the eventful days following the disaster. Two Halifax-based ships hired by the *Titanic's* owners, White Star Line, were loaded with ice, body bags, and rough-hewn coffins before setting out on the grim task of recovering whatever bodies were floating in the icy waters at the site of the sinking, seven hundred miles east of Halifax.

The Karlsen Wharf north of the Halifax Law Courts and next to the Sheraton Hotel and Casino is now home to the red ships of the Karlsen Shipping fleet. But in 1912, the wharf was operations base for the cable repair ship *Mackay-Bennett*, whose cranes proved to be equally capable of hauling bodies from the water. It was from here that *Mackay-Bennett* slipped her lines and headed for sea to search for *Titanic* survivors on April 17, 1912.

A mile to the north of the Maritime Museum of the Atlantic on the waterfront is Her Majesty's Canadian Dockyard, home of the Canadian Navy's Atlantic fleet.

Today, modern frigates, minesweepers, and submarines frequent the

Opposite back-gound photo: Modern skyscrapers, on the Halifax waterfront.

Top inset:
A view of the Halifax waterfront c1906.

Bottom inset:
Jetty No. 4 of the Halifax Dockyard in 1911, showing where a year later, the *Mackay-Bennett* would arrive with the *Titanic* victims.

wharves. But on April 30, 1912, the *Mackay-Bennett*, dubbed the "Death Ship" for her gruesome cargo, arrived at this dockyard (rather than her usual berth at Karlsen Wharf) to unload the 190 *Titanic* bodies pulled from the sea. *Mackay-Bennett* arrived at what was then called North Coaling Wharf No. 4 amid an atmosphere of sombre silence. The wharf had been designated off-limits to both mourners and the press to allow the ship's crew and navy personnel to offload its cargo without interference. Flags in the dockyard where lowered to half-mast as the makeshift coffins and bodies in roughly sewn canvas sacks were transferred to the dock.

Above:
Mackay-Bennett
in drydock.

Opposite:
Karlsen Wharf
today.

Mackay-Bennett
returns to Halifax
with *Titanic's*
dead.

MARITIME MUSEUM OF THE ATLANTIC

Just south of the Karlsen Wharf is the Maritime Museum of the Atlantic, which houses an impressive *Titanic* exhibit.

Included is what is believed to be the only intact *Titanic* deck chair, given to the Rev. Henry Cunningham in recognition of his work with burial and memorial services aboard the cable ship *Minia* during body recovery. One of Cunningham's grandsons donated the chair to the museum. It's made of mahogany and an unidentified hardwood and matches those seen in photographs of *Titanic*.

The museum also has a section of the original ornate wood panelling from the ship's first-class lounge and pieces of the first-class staircase, all plucked from the North Atlantic days after the disaster.

A cribbage board made of recovered wood from the *Titanic*.

The grand staircase is one of several mural-sized photographs on display at the Maritime Museum of the Atlantic's *Titanic* exhibit.

The museum's *Titanic* display features authentic artifacts from the ship, several items once belonging to passengers and many other exhibits related to the ill-fated voyage.

Below: A popular book published shortly after the disaster.

Titanic victim, Charles M. Hays, President of Grand Trunk Railways.

A detail of the mahogany newel post from *Titanic's* grand staircase.

Charles Hays' gloves.

J.J. Astor and a part of his lifebelt.

Above:
A large fragment of the
first class lounge archway was
salvaged by *Minia's* crew members.

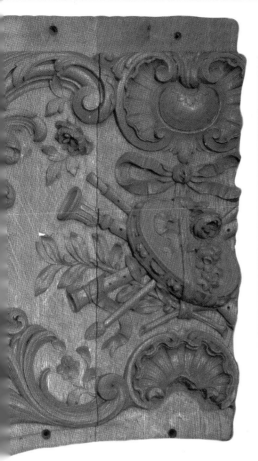

A balustrade section from *Titanic's* grand staircase.

Right: Two visitors examine the newel post detail.

Below: Deck chair from the Titanic.

Maritime Museum of the Atlantic entrance area.

Also in the museum is film footage of *Titanic* leaving her dock in Southampton for her first and last voyage, as well as many photographs of body recovery and people involved in the search. On display is the original handwritten log of *Titanic's* distress messages kept by Robert Hunston, a wireless operator at Cape Race, Nfld. Hunston's family believes he kept the log in case he was called as a witness at an inquiry following the sinking.

Another curious piece of *Titanic* memorabilia at the museum is a cribbage board made by William Parker, *Minia's* carpenter, from a piece of oak salvaged from *Titanic*. In Nova Scotia, the practice of making items from so-called wreck-wood is common. This piece was also donated by Cunningham's family.

Robert Huntington's log; the *Titanic* departing Southampton.

MAYFLOWER CURLING CLUB

Directions: The Mayflower Curling Club was located at what is now the Army-Navy, a surplus goods store on Agricola Street. To get there from downtown Halifax, go west on North Street, which starts on the Halifax side of the Angus L. MacDonald Bridge. Turn right on Agricola Street. The Army-Navy is several blocks on the left. There are currently no Titanic markers for this site.

Horse-drawn hearses and carriages left through the dockyard gates on Water Street to make their way to the temporary morgue established at the Mayflower Curling Club on Agricola Street, in the city's North End. The rink inside the Mayflower was draped in black cloth, a reminder of the terrible event that had taken place.

Immediate family members and relatives of the dead congregated at the rink to identify the bodies of loved ones. One by one family members were escorted into the rink and taken behind a large curtain, where the remains were prepared for viewing, to identify their own among *Titanic's* victims.

Families who had the means arranged to have bodies shipped home for burial. Those who did not arranged for burial in Halifax. Indeed, many of the unidentified second- and third-class passengers and crew came to rest in Halifax's rocky soil.

The Army and Navy Store— the former site of the Mayflower Curling Club on Agricola Street.

The Mayflower Curling Club in 1912. Many *Titanic* victims were kept here in a temporary morgue.

HOME OF HILDA SLAYTER

There are several *Titanic* sites in the central business district of Halifax, including the home of Hilda Slayter. Near the

corner of Argyle and Prince streets is the former home of this young upper-class woman who had been in England to prepare for her wedding. Slayter, whose Halifax home is now the Parish House for St. Paul's Anglican Church, survived *Titanic's* sinking and is thought to be the only *Titanic* survivor buried in Halifax. The disaster did not stop Slayter's wedding plans. She married just two months after *Titanic's* sinking and became Hilda Lacon.

Hilda Slayter's former Halifax home on Argyle Street.

Her grave is located in the Slayter family plot in Camp Hill Cemetery on Summer Street.

Titanic's first class Veranda Café was popular with the younger passengers.

FIVE FISHERMEN— FORMER SITE OF SNOW'S FUNERAL HOME

Half a block to the north of Slayter's house, on Argyle Street, in Halifax's trendy bar district, is the Five Fishermen restaurant, that incorporates the former site of Snow's Funeral Home, where *Titanic's* wealthy victims received special treatment, even in death.

The body of American millionaire John Jacob Astor was prepared at Snow's before his private train car, the *Oceanic*, took his body home to

Today the Five Fishermen Restaurant incorporates a smaller attached building that was the 1912 site of Snow's Funeral home.

the United States. Also taken to Snow's was the body of Charles M. Hays, president of Grand Trunk Railway after he was recovered by *Minia*.

More than forty embalmers from across the Maritimes were kept busy at Snow's and the Mayflower Curling Rink preparing bodies for mass burials.

Snow's staff pose in front of their Argyle Street Funeral home in 1912—on the same block as the Slayter residence.

HALIFAX CHURCHES WHERE FUNERALS WERE HELD

ST. PAUL'S ANGLICAN CHURCH

Directions: St. Paul's Anglican Church is located on one end of Halifax's Grand Parade, the square opposite City Hall.

It was at St. Paul's Church that an overflow service was held for *Titanic's* dead on Sunday, April 21, 1912—the same day

St. Paul's Church on Halifax's Grand Parade, the oldest Protestant church in Canada.

the first of the victims were being recovered at sea. Halifax's only known *Titanic* victim, millionaire George Wright, was a parishioner of St. Paul's and was singled out for attention during the service. The memorial service was attended by many of Halifax's elite, including the Lieutenant Governor of Nova Scotia, members of the provincial government and legislature, Supreme Court justices and other dignitaries.

"The service was a most solemn one and there were not wanting elements of grandeur," reported the *Morning Chronicle* on April 22, 1912. "Its memory will long remain in the minds of those who at this service gave expression of their sorrow. There were few whose hearts were not touched and many were moved to tears."

St. Paul's is the oldest Protestant church in Canada. It was founded by King George II in 1749 and built the following year. Plans for the church were based on St. Peter's Church on Vere Street in London, England. The timbers for St. Paul's were cut in Boston before the American War of Independence and shipped to Halifax.

St. George's Anglican Church

Directions: The Round Church is located on the corner of Brunswick Street and Cornwallis Street, one block west of Barrington Street near the entrance to the Navy Dockyard.

St George's Church, Halifax's famous round church built in 1800.

St. George's Anglican Church, also known as the Round Church, was the site of a funeral for the mysterious baby known as the "Unknown Child" of *Titanic*.

On May 4th, 1912, the church was filled with mourners for the baby, who was later identified as Gosta, the two-year-old son of Swedish emigrant Alma Paulson, another *Titanic* victim. Officiating at the service was Canon Kenneth O. Hind, who had been on the victim recovery ship *Mackay-Bennett* when the boy's body was found. The seventy-five officers and crew of *Mackay-Bennett* were on hand for the funeral, as well as many others in the city who had been deeply touched by the child's fate. At the conclusion of the service, the boy's coffin was covered with flowers and carried from the church by six sailors.

This impressive church was commissioned by Edward, Duke of Kent, Queen Victoria's father. When Edward came to Halifax in 1794, he was the soldier son of George III and commanded his father's forces in Halifax for six years. During that time, he commissioned several famous landmarks, including the Round Church, a round music pavilion on the Bedford Highway, and the town clock on Citadel Hill.

The church, completed after Edward left Halifax, was declared a national historic site in 1990.

Life hasn't been easy for the Round Church. In 1917, five years after *Titanic's* sinking, the Halifax Explosion blew out its windows. The explosion resulted from the wartime collision in the harbour of two ships, the *Mont Blanc* and the *Imo*. The *Mont Blanc* was loaded with enough explosives to create the biggest man-made disaster prior to the dropping of the atom bomb.

On June 2nd, 1994, the church sustained massive damage when three young boys broke in and started a fire that destroyed about 40 per cent of the building. Since then, a major fund-raising campaign has been undertaken to pay for the massive six million dollar restoration bill.

ST. MARY'S BASILICA

Directions: St. Mary's Basilica is located on the corner of Spring Garden Road and Barrington Street, close to downtown Halifax.

St. Mary's Basilica (Cathedral) and its brick Glebe House on Barrington Street c1912.

St. Mary's Basilica, known at the time as St. Mary's Cathedral, was the site of the first actual *Titanic* funerals, on Friday, May 3rd, 1912. Two-and-a-half weeks after the sinking, a service for four unidentified female victims held at the Basilica attracted an overflow congregation, which spilled out onto the street. Notable Roman Catholics from across the province were in attendance, as well as officials from the White Star Line.

GEORGE WRIGHT'S HOUSING DEVELOPMENT

Directions: George Wright's housing development is bounded by South Park Street, Morris Street, and Wright Avenue.

George Wright is thought to be the only Halifax resident who died aboard *Titanic*. Immediately after the disaster, local newspapers were filled with questions about Wright's fate, wondering first if he was aboard and then whether he survived.

Halifax million-aire and Titanic victim, George Wright.

"So far as could be learned, the only Halifax passenger believed to be aboard the *Titanic* was George Wright, whose name appears in the cabled passenger list," says a story in the *Morning Chronicle* on April 15, the day after *Titanic* hit the iceberg. "Mr. Wright has been in Europe for several months, and it is feared that he was on the steamer."

When there was no word of Wright, the city held out hope he may not have been aboard the ill-fated ship. But a week after the disaster, C. W. Frazee, the manager of the Halifax branch of the Royal Bank of Canada, arrived on the White Star Liner *Laurentic* and confirmed that Wright had indeed been on board. Frazee had been in England and had spoken with Wright the morning he left to board *Titanic*.

Wright, who made his millions publishing a worldwide trading directory and gazette, was not seen by any survivors on the night of *Titanic's* sinking.

George Wright's will required that his turreted home on Young Avenue be given to the women of Halifax. It remains the property of the Women's Council of Halifax to this day.

There are no reports of him on deck, either helping with the evacuation or trying to save himself. He was known to be a heavy sleeper and there has been

A first class bedroom aboard the Titanic.

speculation that he may have slept through the entire sinking and drowned in his first-class cabin.

His body was never found.

Wright was known for advancing the cause of the poor and established a housing development in South End Halifax that was revolutionary in the class-conscious times at the turn of the century. Wright's vision housed the wealthy, Halifax's growing middle class, and the working poor on the same block.

A c1906 view of Wright's building on Barrington Street looks much the same today.

The development still exists today. On South Park Street, lofty turreted mansions were the part of the development that housed the wealthy. The more modest houses on Morris Street were designed for Halifax's working class, and the small and tidy wooden row houses on Wright Avenue were for the lower classes.

WRIGHT BUILDING, HALIFAX, N.S.

PUBLIC ARCHIVES OF NOVA SCOTIA

Directions: The Public Archives of Nova Scotia is located on the corner of University Avenue and Robie Street.

There is probably no better place to find *Titanic* documents than at the Public Archives of Nova Scotia.

An extensive collection of the written record of the disaster is there in the form of the original description of the bodies and personal effects, letters, memoranda, and other documents preserved on microfilm. Included are letters of claim to personal effects filed after bodies were viewed at the Mayflower Curling Rink.

One such document is a letter notifying officials in Halifax that body No. 193 had been successfully identified as *Titanic* violinist, John Law (Jock) Hume, who is buried in Fairview Cemetery.

Homes of the well-to-do on South Park Street (top) and workers homes on Wright Avenue (bottom) developed by *Titanic* victim George Wright.

The Public Archives of Nova Scotia.

The letter is dated July 16, 1912 and reads as follows:

Frank F. Wathers esq.
Deputy Provincial Secretary
Halifax, Nova Scotia

Dear Sir:
No. 193 Unidentified
Our Southampton office has advised us that they have been able to identify No. 193 as John Law Hume, a bandsmen of the Titanic from the photograph. We expected this body to be identified, as the uniform and effects indicated that it was that of one of the bandsmen.

The parents of Mr. Hume have asked for the effects, which are of trifling value, and we hope that you may see your way to let us have them, which we will greatly appreciate.

Yours very truly,
For the White Star Line
Harold [illegible]

Letter to the Provincial Secretary from Astor's Attorney.

Halifax, N. S.
Private Car "Oceanic",
April 29/12.

Hon. Provincial Secretary of Nova Scotia,
Halifax, N. S.

Sir,-

I request that you instruct that any personal property found upon the body of the late Colonel John Jacob Astor shall be delivered to me as one of his executors and this letter will be an indemnification as against any person who may hereafter claim to be entitled to the custody or possession of the property.

I have the honour to be,
Sir,
Your obedient servant,

Nicholas Biddle

Another letter on file at the archives is from Nicholas Biddle, attorney for John Jacob Astor. Biddle's letter, written on Astor's private railway car, Oceanic, asks for the release of personal effects.

TITANIC SECRETS REVEALED IN HALIFAX

5

Scientists from the Bedford Institute of Oceanography, on the Dartmouth side of Halifax Harbour, know a good deal about the sunken *Titanic* and her final resting place. They mapped the sea floor at the site of the wreck which was located approximately seven hundred miles east of Halifax.

Through computer-aided analysis of the steel plating in *Titanic's* hull, scientists discovered that the ship's hull was incredibly brittle. When *Titanic* collided with the iceberg, her steel-plated hull didn't bend as it should have; it shattered like glass. At the time of *Titanic's* construction, her steel would have been tested for stress but not for brittleness. What scientists know now is that high sulphur content made the steel used in the ship's construction unsafe. It would never pass inspection today.

Halifax scientists have also been involved in studying the iron drippings (dubbed "rusticles" for their similar appearance to icicles) now covering the ship's hull. They have made a startling discovery about the *Titanic* rusticles: They're alive! Composed of bacteria and other micro-organisms, the rusticles are actually feeding on the steel of *Titanic's* hull.

Within time, the rusticles will consume all that remains of the *Titanic*.

Top and left: The sinking of White Star Line's *SS Atlantic* in 1873, off the south coast of Halifax.

A former White Star ship *Runic* renamed *Imo* was one the colliding ships that caused the explosion in Halifax Harbour in 1917.

OTHER MARINE DISASTERS

6

Halifax has seen more than its fair share of marine disasters since the city's founding in 1749. Hundreds of ships have foundered along the rugged coastline leading into the harbour, and thousands of seafarers have lost their lives to marine tragedies close to its shores.

In 1873, thirty-nine years before *Titanic*'s sinking, another White Star liner, *SS Atlantic*, ran aground in the rock-infested waters near Terence Bay, just outside Halifax Harbour. There were more than one thousand passengers aboard the ship, and less then half of them escaped with their lives.

Many of the victims of that tragedy are buried in a coastline graveyard near the village of Prospect, about twenty-five miles south-west of Halifax. This disaster never received the attention given the *Titanic* tragedy, and many of the graves containing the *SS Atlantic* victims has fallen into disrepair. The sea is again taking its toll:

The great cloud and the devastation caused by the 1917 Halifax explosion.

after severe storms, human bones have been found protruding from the seaward banks of the graveyard.

The wreck of the *SS Atlantic* is

16

a favorite spot for scuba divers as it rests in water only eighty feet deep.

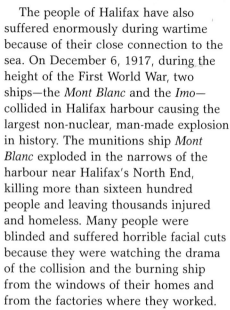

The people of Halifax have also suffered enormously during wartime because of their close connection to the sea. On December 6, 1917, during the height of the First World War, two ships—the *Mont Blanc* and the *Imo*—collided in Halifax harbour causing the largest non-nuclear, man-made explosion in history. The munitions ship *Mont Blanc* exploded in the narrows of the harbour near Halifax's North End, killing more than sixteen hundred people and leaving thousands injured and homeless. Many people were blinded and suffered horrible facial cuts because they were watching the drama of the collision and the burning ship from the windows of their homes and from the factories where they worked.

A terrible winter storm the following day killed many of the injured who died of exposure while trapped in the smoldering rubble of what had been their homes.

Laden with returning troops, *Olympic* arrives in Halifax Harbour in 1919. White Star Line's *Olympic*, *Titanic's* almost identical sister ship, was a frequent visitor to Halifax during the First World War.

At first, it was believed that the explosion was caused by German saboteurs who had targeted Halifax because of its strategic importance as a convoy centre supporting the war effort. An inquiry later determined that the explosion was not planned but resulted from poor navigation and collision avoidance rules.

In an odd coincidence *Titanic's* sister ship, *Olympic*, was anchored in Bedford Basin in Halifax during the Halifax Explosion.

Pictures of *Olympic* are often confused with *Titanic* though *Titanic* weighed slightly more, allowing it to claim the title of "the largest ship afloat."

"TITANIC" — THE MOVIE

7

Halifax's role in the blockbuster movie "Titanic" came almost by chance. James Cameron, the Canadian-born writer and director of the film that has fuelled a worldwide fascination for *Titanic*, needed a site close to the wreck to film key segments. Cameron made twelve dives to the wreck, seven hundred miles east of Halifax, to capture the spectacular footage of *Titanic* that is shown at the beginning of the movie.

"Halifax and St. John's were the two places we looked at when we wanted to mount an expedition to *Titanic*," Cameron told a Halifax newspaper. "It was really a coin toss between the two places."

It turns out that Cameron liked Halifax and decided to shoot the modern-day scenes for the movie in the city in the summer of 1996. The movie opens on a large research ship with the character Brock Lovett, played by Bill Paxton, sending submersibles to the wreck site looking for a priceless lost diamond. Instead he discovers a drawing of a woman wearing the blue diamond heart, which sets the scene for *Titanic's* sinking and the tragic love story of Jack Dawson, played by Leonardo DiCaprio and Rose DeWitt Bukater, played by Kate Winslet.

The research ship in the movie was actually the Russian research vessel, *Keldysh*, chartered by Cameron. The modern-day scenes were filmed on the Dartmouth side of Halifax Harbour for eighteen days in July and August of 1996. The story of *Titanic's* voyage and sinking was filmed at Rosarito Beach, Mexico, a three-hour drive south of Los Angeles.

The Halifax shoot may have been a minor part of the movie, but it became famous because of a bizarre incident that occurred during its conclusion. About

LEONARDO DiCAPRIO   KATE WINSLET

A JAMES CAMERON FILM

TITANIC

Promotional poster for "Titanic."

eighty members of the cast and crew—including Cameron and actor Bill Paxton—became ill after eating lobster chowder at a wrap-up party. It was later learned that the chowder was laced with a drug called phencyclidine, more commonly known as angel dust. Police have yet to find the culprit.

AUTHORS' TITANIC STORIES

8

ALAN JEFFERS' STORY OF TITANIC ARTIFACTS

There are probably hundreds of people in and around Halifax who have a story about *Titanic* from relatives or whose homes contain some of the hundreds of souvenirs picked up by the sailors of the cable ships *Mackay-Bennett* or *Minia* during body recovery. But every once in a while, a new *Titanic* artifact surfaces. This is a story about artifacts that surfaced but disappeared again. Several years ago while working as a reporter for The Canadian Press news agency, I had a small office in the basement of Province House, a century-old building that is Canada's oldest seat of government.

One day, a careless security guard left a door next to my office open. I and several other reporters couldn't resist the temptation to explore the dank and dusty basement of this historic building for whatever lost treasures that might be inside. We went through the door into a modern-looking room with locked cabinets—nothing too exciting.

Another doorway led us into another room, which appeared far less travelled. There were some boxes of papers on shelves, but again nothing that caught our interest.

Still another doorway led into a third room. On the shelves were dust-covered boxes with more documents and another doorway into a fourth room with a vault. Now things were getting interesting. Here we found some marvelous remnants of a bygone age.

A ledger contained handwritten attendance and expense accounts of members of the Executive Council in the 1940s when Angus L. Macdonald was premier of Nova Scotia. A stack of phonograph records still in their packaging was addressed to the Provincial Secretary. Inside, according to the label on the cover, was a recording of the 1940 ceremony marking the one hundredth anniversary of Nova Scotia's place as the

Province House in Halifax, Canada's oldest seat of government.

birthplace of responsible government in British North America.

It was the next discovery that sent chills up my spine. I picked up a dusty accordion-style folder bearing a note fastened with an elastic band. On the note were the words: Artifacts from *Titanic*.

Nervously, I peered inside. The folder contained some kind of receipts from the Bank of Finland with the name Gustafsson on them as well as some other papers.

After leaving the basement, I reported the find to officials at Province House, who in turn called in archivists from the

Public Archives of Nova Scotia. They came and carried off all the material from the basement rooms.

I neglected to follow up on whatever happened to the lost *Titanic* artifacts until starting the research for this book. I was surprised to learn that no one at the archives has any recollection of the find. Neither do they have the *Titanic* artifacts from that accordion folder.

Wanting to be sure, I checked again at Province House; the rooms had been cleared of everything. I was assured that officials from the archives had removed all the contents of the mysterious rooms but where the artifacts are today is still a mystery. How they got in the basement of Province House is not.

It turns out that it was not unusual for officials to store items of value in that remote and hidden basement vault over the years. The legislature's librarian, Margaret Murphy, told me that she had once seen body bags from the 1917 Halifax Explosion in the same basement.

The name Gustafsson on the papers I had seen provided a clue to the authenticity of the documents. There were four people named Gustafsson on board *Titanic* travelling as third class passengers. Three died, but the only body recovered was that of Anders Vilhelm Gustafsson, a thirty-seven-year-old farmer heading to America for a construction job.

The cable steamer *Mackay-Bennett* found the remains of Gustafsson, a native of Lovisa in Southern Finland, on April 23. He was buried at sea, but his personal effects were returned to Halifax aboard *Mackay-Bennett* and probably made their way to the Mayflower Curling Rink, which served as a makeshift morgue for *Titanic's* dead.

When the morgue was closed,

between $50,000 and $75,000 worth of valuables were taken from the rink to the office of the Provincial Treasurer.

According to the meticulous *Titanic* records kept by the crew aboard *Mackay-Bennett*, Gustafsson was wearing a dark suit, grey socks, a shirt and pants with the initials A. W. C. on them when he was pulled from the water. In his pockets were a watch and chain, a knife and comb, keys and a purse containing twenty-one dollars in bills along with some coins.

The *Titanic* artifacts I discovered had remained in the dingy basement of Province House for over three-quarters of a century, undisturbed by time. They resurfaced briefly but are now lost again.

ROB GORDON'S GREAT AUNT ETHEL—TITANIC SURVIVOR

Many people in Halifax have a connection to the *Titanic*: friends and relatives who were aboard or who joined the search for the survivors or helped with the burials.

I, too, have a *Titanic* connection.

It's a story of love and honour, tragedy and loss. In 1912, my grandfather's brother, Crawford Gordon, fell in love with a young Winnipeg woman named Ethel Fortune. Crawford asked Ethel to marry him and she agreed.

As many well-to-do English-speaking Canadians did at the time, Ethel travelled to England to buy her trousseau. She was accompanied by her mother, Mary, two sisters Mabel and Alice, brother Charles and her father, Mark.

Stories passed down in my family tell of how excited the Fortunes were about the trip and how lucky they felt to get first-class tickets aboard *Titanic*, the grandest, most luxurious ship ever built.

I can well imagine the horror and shock the Fortune family felt when *Titanic's* starboard bow crashed into that North Atlantic iceberg on April 14. Life for them would never be the same.

Ethel, her sisters and mother climbed into Lifeboat No. 10. Just as the boat was about to be lowered by the crew members, the Fortune women tossed Mark and Charles their jewellery and valuables. Sadly, that was the last Ethel saw of her father and brother. Mark and Charles went down with the ship; their bodies were never recovered.

Titanic survivor Ethel Fortune, seated to the right and wearing sunglasses. Her husband Crawford Gordon is the man standing to the left.

The Fortune women had unusual stories about their rescue to tell their grandchildren. As their lifeboat pulled away from *Titanic*, Ethel felt something brush against her leg. Under the lifeboat bench she discovered an Asian cook who had stowed away aboard the boat. She also saw a man aboard who was dressed as a woman-wearing a bonnet, a veil, skirt and blouse.

A newspaper account from 1912 quotes Ethel's mother as saying that the lifeboat was "terribly overcrowded" and that crew members who had been assigned to Lifeboat No. 10 were transferred to another boat, leaving one only professional seafarer to steer No. 10 to the rescue ship *Carpathia*.

The Fortune women also witnessed several very controversial and disturbing events both aboard the lifeboat and on

Titanic herself. They saw crew members fire shots above the heads of "struggling and shrieking" steerage passengers who were trying to get into lifeboats. Ethel reported that some crew members lowered their guns and fired directly into the crowd. Although experts say the stories of crew members shooting steerage passengers in the final moments before *Titanic* sank have never been confirmed, Ethel and her mother say they saw one man wounded in the arm. Ethel's word is good enough for me.

The Fortune women also witnessed what became known as "the last plunge of the *Titanic*." Just before the ship disappeared from view, people struggled to clear the decks. The bandsmen, they said, kept playing to the last. The final sound they heard from the great ship was the band playing the sombre hymn "Nearer My God to Thee."

The *Titanic* disaster didn't stop Ethel and Crawford's wedding plans. After a time of mourning they married and eventually had two sons, including one named Crawford Jr., who later became the Chief Executive Officer of the AVRO Company, the designer and builder of the famous Canadian supersonic fighter jet, the Arrow.

Actor Dan Ackroyd played Crawford Gordon, son of a *Titanic* survivor, in the 1996 Canadian feature film "The Arrow."

My grandfather and Crawford Gordon Sr.'s brother, William Verner Gordon, is buried in the Fairview Cemetery in Halifax, just a few feet from the graves where the remains of 121 *Titanic* victims lie. I often wonder as I walk among the graves of the unknown victims if one of them could be Mark or Charles Fortune.

APPENDIX:
TITANIC HALIFAX
TIMELINE

All times are local to the event.

★ 1907   The idea of *Titanic* is born. Plans are made to build the greatest luxury liner in the world.

★ 1908   Fifteen thousand Belfast shipyard workers at the Harland and Woolf Shipyard lay down *Titanic's* keel.

★ 1911   *Titanic's* 46,328 ton hull rolls down the ways in Belfast.

★ April 10, 1912   *Titanic's* maiden sailing day.
• 9:30-11:30 A.M.   Passengers begin streaming up gangway in Southampton.
• Noon   *Titanic* slips her lines from the dock and begins her first and only voyage.
• 6:30 P.M.   *Titanic* drops anchor in Cherbourg, France where more passengers are ferried to the ship in small boats.
• 8:10 P.M.   *Titanic* hauls anchor and steams for Queenstown, Ireland.

★ April 11, 1912, 1:30 P.M. *Titanic* boards more passengers in Queenstown and heads to sea. Destination: New York.

★ April 12, 1912   *Titanic* steams at speed toward New York. Voyage uneventful.

★ April 13, 1912   Cunard liner *Carpathia* leaves New York for Naples.

Thomas Andrews, managing director of Hartland and Woolf perished in the disaster.

The *Titanic* off the coast of France.

★ April 14, 1912   *Titanic*'s wireless operators receive several warnings of icebergs in the area.

• 11:40 P.M.   Lookouts high atop *Titanic*'s crows-nest see icebergs dead ahead. *Titanic* rams iceberg with starboard bow.

• 11:50 P.M.   Water pours into *Titanic*'s hull. Within minutes water in bow reaches the fourteen foot mark. Midnight   *Titanic* Captain Edward John Smith gives order to send out first distress signal.

Titanic's last message.

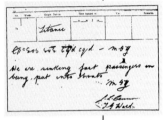

★ April 15, 1912

• 12:05 A.M.   *Titanic* sends message that she had "struck iceberg." Orders are given for deckhands to uncover lifeboats, which have room for only half the 2,228 passengers.

• 12:25 A.M.   Women and children begin climbing into *Titanic*'s lifeboats. *Carpathia*, now fifty-eight nautical miles south-east of the area, picks up *Titanic*'s distress signal.

• 12:45 A.M.   *Titanic*'s first lifeboats lowered. First distress rockets fired by *Titanic*'s crew.

• 1:06 A.M.   *Titanic* sends message: "We are putting women off in boats."

• 1:40 A.M.   Most lifeboats rowing away from badly listing *Titanic*. Those left aboard begin streaming to stern.

• 2:05 A.M.   Last lifeboat leaves *Titanic*; 705 people escape and 1,523 are stranded aboard sinking ship.

• 2:17 A.M.   Captain Smith tells crew that it is "every man for himself." Last distress signal sent from *Titanic*. One of *Titanic*'s four funnels crashes to the deck, killing several people.

• 2:18 A.M.   *Titanic*'s lights blink once and go out. The ship breaks in two. Bow sinks.

Titanic's Captain Edward John Smith.

- 2:20 A.M. Stern sinks. *Titanic* is gone forever, killing 1,523.
- 4:10 A.M. *Carpathia* picks up first *Titanic* lifeboat and survivors.

★ April 15, 1912 Mixed wireless signals lead world to believe *Titanic* passengers are safe and ship is being towed to Halifax.

★ April 16, 1912 News of full extent of tragedy spreads after contact made with *Carpathia*.

★ April 17, 1912, 12:35 P.M. Cable ship *Mackay-Bennett* leaves Karlsen Wharf in Halifax to search for bodies.

★ April 18, 1912, 9:00 A.M. *Carpathia* arrives in New York with 705 *Titanic* survivors.

★ April 20, 1912, Noon *Mackay-Bennett* Captain F. H. Lardner asks other ships for reports of wreckage.
- 8:00 P.M. *Mackay-Bennett* arrives at sinking site.

A boat from the *Mackay-Bennett* finds the lifeboat Collapsible B overturned.

★ April 21, 1912 *Mackay-Bennett* pulls fifty-one bodies from the sea, including Gosta Paulson, Unknown Child of *Titanic*, and fugitive Michel Navratil. Memorial service on forecastle deck, burials at sea.

★ April 22, 1912 5:30 A.M. Search resumes. *Mackay-Bennett* finds *Titanic* lifeboat Collapsible B overturned with a hole in side. Twenty-seven bodies recovered, including John Jacob Astor.
- Near Midnight Cable ship *Minia* leaves Halifax to join search.

★ April 23, 1912   *Mackay-Bennett* finds eighty-seven bodies during a fourteen hour search.
• 8:00 P.M.   Burials at sea.

★ April 24 and 25, 1912   Fog and rough weather hamper search.

★ April 26, 1912, 12:45 A.M.   *Minia* arrives alongside *Mackay-Bennett*.

The *Minia*.

• 6:15 A.M.   *Minia* lowers small boat and transfers embalming fluid and supplies to *Mackay-Bennett*.
• Noon   Fourteen bodies recovered. *Mackay-Bennett* returns to Halifax after recovering 306 bodies; 116 buried at sea, 190 still aboard. *Minia* recovers 11 bodies.

★ April 27, 1912   Gale and fog slow *Minia*. One body recovered.
•2:20 A.M.   Francis Dyke, *Minia*'s temporary wireless operator, begins letter to his mother.

★ April 28, 1912   *Minia* recovers one body. Churchgoers in Halifax asked not to congregate at waterfront when *Mackay-Bennett* arrives with bodies.

★ April 30, 1912, 9:30 A.M.   *Mackay-Bennett* arrives in Halifax Harbour. Stops at George's Island to collect officials before tying up at North Coaling Wharf No. 4.
• 1:00 P.M.   *Mackay-Bennett* unloading completed. Bodies moved to temporary morgue at Mayflower Curling Club.

★ May 2, 1912   Bodies at Mayflower prepared for burial. Rabbi Jacob Walter visits rink for inspection; identifies nine victims as Jewish.

★ May 3, 1912　*Minia* abandons search for bodies. Fisheries ship *Montmagny* leaves Sorel, Que., for Halifax.

• 9:30 A.M.　Funeral services at St. Mary's Cathedral for four unidentified women.

• 11:00 A.M.　Memorial service at Brunswick Street Methodist Church for fifty victims, mostly unidentified crew.

• 3:00 P.M.　Grave-side service at Fairview Cemetery. Ten bodies discovered missing, later found at Baron de Hirsch Jewish Cemetery. Ten buried at Baron de Hirsch; disputed ten returned to Mayflower Rink. Four buried at Mount Olivet Cemetery.

★ May 4, 1912　Funeral at St. George's Anglican Church for Gosta Paulson, the Unknown Child of *Titanic*. Burial at Fairview.

★ May 6, 1912, 2:00 A.M.　*Minia* arrives outside Halifax Harbour.

• 7:00 A.M.　*Minia* ties up at North Coaling Wharf No. 4 to unload bodies. Thirty-three buried in Fairview.

Carriage house for Snow's Funeral Home.

Montmagny arrives in Halifax and picks up undertakers and supplies, leaves to search for bodies.

★ May 8, 1912　Seven bodies buried in Mount Olivet Cemetery.

★ May 10, 1912　Montmagny recovers three bodies. Thirty-two buried in Fairview. Makeshift morgue closes at Mayflower Curling Club.

TITANIC SHIP FACTS

★ *Titanic* was designed to carry thirty-two lifeboats. The number was later reduced to twenty because the White Star Line thought too many lifeboats spoiled her clean, streamlined look.

★ *Titanic's* home port was Southampton. She was registered in Liverpool, England.

★ *Titanic* could hold as many as thirty-five hundred people.

★ A first-class ticket aboard *Titanic* cost $4,350—about $50,000 today.

★ *Titanic* cost $7.5 million to build in 1912—about $500 million today.

★ May 11, 1912   *Montmagny* recovers one body, buried at sea. Two bodies buried in Fairview.

★ May 13, 1912   *Montmagny* arrives in Louisbourg, N.S. Three bodies transferred to Halifax by train.

★ May 15, 1912   Privately owned ship *Algerine* leaves St. John's, Nfld., to search for bodies. Finds James McGrady, the last to be recovered. Body of Serrando Ovies y Rodrigues is exhumed from Fairview Cemetery and reburied in Mount Olivet Cemetery.

★ May 16, 1912   Marcelle Navratil reunited with her sons, the *Titanic* Orphans, in New York.

★ May 19, 1912   *Montmagny* abandons search.

★ May 20, 1912   Two bodies from *Montmagny* buried in Mount Olivet and Fairview Cemeteries.

★ June 11, 1912   James McGrady's body arrives in Halifax.

★ June 12, 1912   James McGrady is buried in Fairview Cemetery.